The Future of Work

MANAGEMENT IN DIGITAL TIMES

Edited by Piotr Olaf Żylicz

VOLUME 4

Krzysztof Wasilewski and Tomasz Królikowski (eds.)

The Future of Work. An Interdisciplinary Approach

PETER LANG
Berlin · Bruxelles · Chennai · Lausanne · New York · Oxford

Bibliographic information published by the Deutsche Nationalbibliothek
The Deutsche Nationalbibliothek lists this publication in the Deutsche Nationalbibliografie; detailed bibliographic data are available on the Internet at https://dnb.dnb.de.

Library of Congress Cataloging-in-Publication Data
A CIP catalog record for this book has been applied for at the Library of Congress.

Publikacja sfinansowana zgodnie z założeniami projektu Politechniki Koszalińskiej „Politechnika Koszalińska aktywnym członkiem EU4Dual" (umowa o dofinansowanie nr BPI/WUE/2024/1/00009/U/00001) ze środków europejskich z Funduszu Europejskiego dla Rozwoju Społecznego w ramach projektu Narodowej Agencji Wymiany Akademickiej pn. „Wsparcie sojuszy Uniwersytetów Europejskich" o numerze FERS.01.05-IP.08-0219/23.

Fundusze Europejskie dla Rozwoju Społecznego
Rzeczpospolita Polska
Dofinansowane przez Unię Europejską
NAWA Narodowa Agencja Wymiany Akademickiej

This publication is a result of the Lighthouse Research Initiative "Interdisciplinarity in Social Sciences. A European Way of Life", led by the Koszalin University of Technology – Digital Humanities and New Media Lab, within the EU4Dual European University.

DEUTSCH POLNISCHE WISSENSCHAFTS STIFTUNG | POLSKO NIEMIECKA FUNDACJA NA RZECZ NAUKI

Artykuł pt. "AI and new technologies in local journalism in Poland and Germany: Case study of local media in West Pomerania and Baden-Württemberg" powstał i został opublikowany w ramach projektu wspieranego przez Polsko-Niemiecką Fundację na rzecz Nauki/ Artikel "AI and new technologies in local journalism in Poland and Germany: Case study of local media in West Pomerania and Baden-Württemberg" wurde im Rahmen des von Polnisch-Deutsche Wissenschaftsstiftung unterstützten Projekts erstellt und veröffentlicht.

ISSN 2699-3511
ISBN 978-3-631-95004-3 (Print)
ISBN 978-3-631-95005-0 (ePDF)
ISBN 978-3-631-95545-1 (ePUB)
DOI 10.3726/b23977

PETER LANG
open

Published by Peter Lang GmbH, Berlin, Germany

info@peterlang.com

This publication has been peer reviewed.

www.peterlang.com

Contact for General Product Safety Regulation (GPSR): gpsr@peterlang.com

Contents

List of Figures vii

List of Tables ix

AI and new technologies in local journalism in Poland and Germany: Case study of local media in West Pomerania and Baden-Württemberg 1
Hanna Tsesta, Yvonne Zajontz, Krzysztof Wasilewski

Industry 5.0 and human-centric workplaces 21
Brice Miard, Maxime Daniel, Nadine Couture

Study on the influence of repeated use of PA12 powder on the evolution of mechanical properties, morphology, and dimensional stability of parts produced using SLS technology 29
Sebastian Banucha, Tomasz Królikowski, Sebastian Pecolt, Andrzej Błażejewski, Piotr Zmuda Trzebiatowski, Rafał Wątor

AI and gender, racial, and ethnic inequalities in workspaces 49
Dominika Liszkowska

Algorithms, security, and civil defence 65
Krzysztof Kaczmarek, Natalia Moch, Małgorzata Żmigrodzka, Dorota Sylwia Majewicz

Reworking the local public sector? Mapping research trends and challenges related to the new technologies 77
Ewa Włodyka

Digital storytelling as a space of learning creativity in HE 105
Marta Gliniecka

Human rights in the age of digital surveillance: Challenges for the Strasbourg standard – selected issues 119
Maria Ochwat

AI as a co-creator: How artificial intelligence is transforming the gaming industry 137
Igor Walczak

Figures

Sebastian Banucha, Tomasz Królikowski, Sebastian Pecolt, Andrzej Błażejewski, Piotr Zmuda Trzebiatowski, Rafał Wątor
Study on the influence of repeated use of PA12 powder on the evolution of mechanical properties, morphology, and dimensional stability of parts produced using SLS technology
Figure 1: Sintratec Kit SLS printer used in the research 33
Figure 2: Technical drawing of the test sample compliant with PN-EN ISO 527-2 34
Figure 3: CAD visualisation of the test sample 34
Figure 4: Vibratory sieve used for powder recovery after each cycle 35
Figure 5: Type 1BA sample (PA12) clamped in the jaws of the Zwick Z010 TN testing machine during the static tensile test 36
Figure 6: Change in average tensile strength (UTS) over ten recycling cycles 38
Figure 7: Change in average elongation at break over ten recycling cycles 39
Figure 8: Change in average yield strength over ten recycling cycles 39
Figure 9: Change in standard deviation of stresses (UTS) over ten recycling cycles 40
Figure 10: Comparison of SEM images: (left) fresh PA12 powder (Cycle 1), (right) PA12 powder after ten recycling cycles (Cycle 10). Visible surface degradation and grain agglomeration 41
Figure 11: Change (decrease) in the average cross-sectional area of samples over ten recycling cycles, indicating increasing material shrinkage 42

Tables

Sebastian Banucha, Tomasz Królikowski, Sebastian Pecolt, Andrzej Błażejewski, Piotr Zmuda Trzebiatowski, Rafał Wątor
Study on the influence of repeated use of PA12 powder on the evolution of mechanical properties, morphology, and dimensional stability of parts produced using SLS technology
Table 1: Specification of PA12 material (Sintratec) used for testing 32
Table 2: Summary results of mechanical properties of PA12 samples in ten recycling cycles 37

Ewa Włodyka
Reworking the local public sector? Mapping research trends and challenges related to the new technologies
Table 1: Results from repetitorium (database of scientific articles) and searched keywords 85
Table 2: Selected topics by geographical area 88

Marta Gliniecka
Digital storytelling as a space of learning creativity in HE
Table 1: The use of AI by students from two universities to create digital storytelling 113

AI and new technologies in local journalism in Poland and Germany: Case study of local media in West Pomerania and Baden-Württemberg

Hanna Tsesta[1], *Yvonne Zajontz*[2], *Krzysztof Wasilewski*[3]

The global release of ChatGPT in November 2022, followed by the rapid proliferation of other generative artificial intelligence platforms, has marked a turning point in the relationship between journalism and automated technologies. While some newsrooms had experimented with artificial intelligence for tasks such as data analysis, content recommendation, or newsletter distribution prior to this moment, the diffusion of large language models has fundamentally altered both the scope and accessibility of AI tools within media organisations. Over the past three years, generative systems have become an increasingly integral component of journalistic work worldwide, supporting activities ranging from newsgathering and content production to audience engagement (Borchardt, 2025). By automating routine and time-consuming tasks, these technologies potentially allow journalists to devote greater attention to investigative and analytical work. At the same time, however, generative AI has raised profound concerns related to the production and circulation of disinformation, the amplification of hate speech, and the erosion of public trust in journalism. These challenges are further compounded by evidence that a growing number of users increasingly rely on platforms such as ChatGPT, rather than established news outlets, as sources of information about current affairs (Simon, Nielsen, & Fletcher, 2025).

Against this backdrop, existing scholarship on AI and journalism has expanded rapidly. Much of this literature, however, focuses on technologically advanced, well-resourced news organisations, mostly in the United States or Western Europe, often emphasising technological capabilities rather than journalists' situated perceptions and organisational contexts. Far less attention has been paid to local journalism, where limited resources, closer

1 Doctoral School, Koszalin University of Technology
2 Duale Hochschule Baden-Württemberg (Heilbronn)
3 Koszalin University of Technology

relationships with audiences, and stronger organisational constraints may significantly shape both opportunities and risks associated with AI adoption. As a result, important questions remain unanswered regarding how journalists operating outside major media centres perceive generative AI and assess its relevance for their professional practices.

This study addresses this gap by examining journalists' perceptions of generative artificial intelligence through the lens of the innovation readiness framework. Innovation readiness emphasises the extent to which individuals and organisations are prepared to adopt new technologies, taking into account not only technical infrastructure, but also skills, attitudes, organisational cultures, and perceived risks and benefits (Zerfaß, 2005). Applied to journalism, this perspective makes it possible to move beyond deterministic accounts of technological change and instead analyse how readiness for innovation is shaped by professional norms, institutional arrangements, and broader socio-economic conditions.

Empirically, the paper draws on a series of semi-structured interviews conducted with local media professionals in two distinct European regions: West Pomerania (Poland) and Baden-Württemberg (Germany). Both regions are characterised by a distinct local media landscape and a strong integration of journalism into regional public spheres. At the same time, local media in both contexts face similar challenges, such as managing limited resources, navigating digital transformation processes, adapting to changing user habits, and dealing with declining subscriber numbers (de-Lima-Santos & Ceron, 2022; Loosen et al., 2020). These commonalities provide a suitable basis for a comparative examination of the perception of generative artificial intelligence in local journalism under varying structural and economic-geographical conditions. West Pomerania can be characterised as an economic and technological semi-periphery, shaped by post-socialist transformation and comparatively limited media resources, whereas Baden-Württemberg represents one of the most technologically advanced and economically prosperous regions in the European Union. This comparative design allows for an examination of how different levels of organisational capacity, technological infrastructure, and professional support structures influence journalists' innovation readiness with regard to generative AI. The study is guided by three research questions:

Q1: How do local journalists perceive the role of generative artificial intelligence in their everyday professional practices?

Q2: How do these perceptions differ between journalists operating in semi-peripheral and core regions of the European media landscape?
Q3: Which organisational, professional, and technological factors shape journalists' readiness to adopt and use AI-based tools?

The contribution of this paper is threefold. First, it foregrounds local journalism as a crucial yet under-researched site of technological transformation, highlighting how proximity to audiences and resource constraints affect innovation readiness. Second, by comparing a semi-peripheral and a core European region, the study introduces a spatially sensitive perspective into debates on AI and journalism. Third, by employing qualitative interviews, it provides in-depth insights into journalists' attitudes, concerns, and expectations – dimensions that remain insufficiently explored in predominantly quantitative research on AI in media environments.

Literature review

According to the systematic literature review, the contemporary scholarship on artificial intelligence and journalism can be broadly divided into four thematic strands. The first strand focuses on the ethical challenges associated with the introduction of AI and related technologies in media organisations. For instance, Dierickx et al. (2024) highlight issues of accuracy, fairness, and transparency in data-driven newsrooms. Related concerns regarding the legal risks of automated journalism and algorithmic systems are addressed by Lewis et al. (2018) and Peña-Fernández et al. (2023). While the former examines the potential for algorithms to generate libellous news content, the latter employs a systematic literature review to analyse two decades of research on AI implementation in the media, with particular attention to empirical studies and the social and epistemological challenges arising from AI adoption.

The second strand addresses the implications of AI for journalistic education and professional training. The growing number of questions raised by the integration of AI into newsrooms has generated calls for new approaches to journalism education. Wenger et al. (2025) apply the theory of disruptive innovation to examine how emerging technologies are reshaping media education. Similarly, Lopezosa et al. (2023) analyse the incorporation of generative AI into journalist training, emphasising the need for supervised and transparent use of AI tools alongside the reinforcement of core journalistic values. A comparable perspective is offered by Luttrell et al. (2020), who underline the importance of integrating new technologies into media literacy initiatives aimed at both media producers and media consumers.

The third strand comprises studies examining how computational automation and algorithmic systems transform newsroom practices and professional roles. As early as 2013, Gynnild analysed the adoption of new technologies in media organisations, distinguishing three approaches: newsroom-driven, academic, and entrepreneurial. One of her key findings was that technological innovation not only enables new journalistic practices but also reshapes journalists' ways of thinking. Building on this line of inquiry, Schapals and Porlezza (2020) investigate whether automated journalism challenges or reinforces traditional journalistic roles. More recently, Ruiz et al. (2023) explore the emergence of so-called synthetic media, in which content is produced entirely through algorithmic processes.

The fourth strand encompasses research on data-driven journalism and broader patterns of adaptation within the media industry. Foundational discussions of journalism in the era of big data and AI can be found in the work of Howard (2014) and Hammond (2017). According to Loosen et al. (2020), the introduction of AI represents a profound transformation of reporting practices. Several studies have examined how this transformation is experienced by journalists and audiences alike. For example, de-Lima Santos and Ceron (2022) assess the news industry's readiness to adopt AI tools, while Gutiérrez-Caneda et al. (2023) conduct an experimental study involving twelve journalists with no prior exposure to advanced technological tools to evaluate whether and how AI accelerates journalistic work. Other scholars focus on audience engagement with algorithmically produced news, analysing patterns of interaction and reception (Ndlovu, 2024; Parasie & Dagiral, 2013).

Innovation readiness framework

The innovation readiness framework is used to evaluate an organisation's capability to develop and adapt new ideas, products or technologies. Innovation readiness describes the extent to which individuals and organisations are capable of and willing to adopt new technologies and use them effectively (Zerfaß, 2005). According to van den Hoed et al. (2022, p. 2), "organisations encounter difficulties in structuring their innovation processes, while existing procedures and regulations often restrain innovative initiatives; moving to a state of readiness for innovation differs from preparing to introduce a specific innovation." Challenges that may block an organisation from employing new technologies are manifold as some derive from an organisation structure while others can result from human beliefs and sets of values (Webster & Gardner, 2019, p. 1233). As such, innovation readiness takes place on three levels: organisational culture, climate, and capability. Organisational culture encompasses shared values and norms; the organisational climate refers to the perceived support for innovation; and organisational capabilities refer to the available skills and resources needed to implement new technologies (van den Hoed et al., 2022).

Many research studies on innovation readiness framework focus on organisational implications while leaving out the human factor. However, as Salazar and Russi-Vigoya (2021) point out, "understanding the human and technology relationship is imperative, especially in complex systems that could end the human life or end the mission." Whereas organisational structure and culture are important for the introduction of innovation, it is human ability to absorb these changes or reject them (Zammuto & O'Connor, 1992) that play an essential role in this process. This is especially important in media organisations whose success depends on journalists' skills to uncover news and make it accessible for large publics. At the same time, journalists are expected to acquire new digital competences that affect news production, as well as distribution and consumption (Cózar et al., 2022). Therefore, innovation readiness is especially complex in media organisations and as such demands further research. Against this backdrop, the innovation readiness approach serves as an analytical framework for examining the extent to which local journalists in West Pomerania and Baden-Württemberg are prepared for the use of generative artificial intelligence, and which factors influence their willingness to adopt these technologies.

Methodology

The systematic literature review reveals several persistent gaps in contemporary research on artificial intelligence in journalism. Existing studies predominantly concentrate either on the organisational adoption of AI within media companies or on the capacity of automated journalism to substitute traditional, human-centred journalistic practices. Considerably less attention has been paid to journalists' own perceptions, attitudes, and everyday experiences of working with AI-driven tools and related technologies. As a result, the subjective and professional dimensions of technological change in newsrooms remain underexplored, despite their importance for understanding the social acceptance, ethical evaluation, and practical implementation of innovation.

In addition, much of the existing scholarship focuses on media organisations located in the United States and other technologically advanced countries, thereby marginalising contexts situated in what world-systems theory defines as technological semi-peripheries (Wallerstein, 1974). Poland represents a particularly relevant case in this regard. Although the country underwent democratic transformation in the 1990s, joined the European Union, and has achieved notable economic growth, it continues to lag behind Europe's technological core in terms of innovation capacity, digital infrastructure, and research and development intensity. These structural conditions shape not only the availability of AI tools in newsrooms but also journalists' expectations, anxieties, and strategies of adaptation.

Against this background, the present study aims to comparatively examine innovation readiness in local media organisations operating in two contrasting regional contexts: West Pomerania in Poland, which exemplifies many characteristics of a technological semi-periphery, and Baden-Württemberg in Germany, one of Europe's most technologically and economically advanced regions. By juxtaposing these cases, the study seeks to illuminate how regional structural conditions intersect with professional cultures to shape journalists' engagement with AI and related technologies.

Methodologically, the study employs semi-structured interviews with journalists working in local media outlets in both regions. While quantitative research in journalism studies often prioritises organisational indicators and measurable outputs, qualitative approaches – particularly in-depth interviews – enable access to less visible aspects of professional practice, such as normative orientations, tacit knowledge, and everyday coping strategies (Belina, 2023). The interviews were analysed using qualitative content analysis as described by Philipp Mayring (2015) and drawing on the structured content analysis approach outlined by Udo Kuckartz (2018). This approach enables a systematic, rule-based analysis of textual material and the identification of key thematic deductive and inductive categories. While the main categories were developed on the basis of the research questions and the interview guide, the differentiation of subcategories was carried out inductively on the basis of the text material (Mayring, 2015).

The research process involved the development of a structured interview guide and pilot testing to ensure clarity and thematic coherence (Doody & Noonan, 2013). The interview guide was based on the research questions and covered different topics such as the use of AI in everyday work, perceived opportunities and risks, and organisational framework conditions. Interviews were conducted either online, using the Zoom platform, or in person, depending on availability and logistical constraints (Basch et al., 2020). In total, five journalists from local media in Baden-Württemberg and six journalists from West Pomerania participated in the study. The interviews lasted between approximately 40 and 73 minutes. Interviews were conducted in German and Polish, transcribed verbatim, and subsequently translated into English to facilitate collaborative analysis within the research team. The analysis was carried out in several stages, beginning with open coding, followed by the formation of thematic categories and their consolidation in line with qualitative content analysis. The main identified categories are the use of AI, perceptions of AI, effects on work processes, opportunities, risks, organisational conditions and future expectations

Research

West Pomerania

In total, six journalists from West Pomerania were interviewed. The cohort comprised four women and two men. The age span included three persons in the age 20–35 and three over 35; five interviewees worked in traditional media organisations, that is radio, printed press and TV whereas two worked in online media. Each interview lasted between 40 and 60 minutes.

All interviewees reported developing an interest in journalism at an early stage of their education. Four had completed internships in local media organisations while still in high school, whereas two entered journalism during their university studies. The motivations underlying their career choices included a desire to help others, a strong interest in local affairs, and a willingness to contribute to positive change within their immediate social environment. As one respondent explained:

> I've always liked being in contact with people, and this job is based on contact with people, so that's really the essence of it. And when I saw that there was space to work with people in a way that genuinely interested me, it was obvious – it just clicked straight away (Interview PL 1).

Importantly, the interviewees consistently emphasised that their decision to work in local media was a deliberate one, grounded in their perception of journalism as a form of community service. To support this argument, one of the interviewees established her own online news service as in her opinion, her hometown was lacking independent local media.

In general, the interviewees expressed positive opinions about AI and new technologies in journalism. However, there are differences in how they understand these technologies. For one of them new technologies meant simple resources, such as word processors and digital recorders. Still others defined them as computer-automated tools, specifically automatic transcription software or editorial correction. For all of them, new technologies make journalism much faster. According to one interviewee,

> when there was a printed newspaper, journalists working in print always had a built-in delay. We had that one-day lag: if something happened on Tuesday, we wrote about it for Wednesday, whereas our colleagues in television and radio had to report on it immediately – especially once the internet appeared (Interview PL 2).

The interviewees pointed out the lack of organisational regulations concerning AI and new technologies. Although they expressed a largely positive attitude towards the employment of computer-automated resources in newsrooms, in their opinion this process has to be controlled by media organisations. Otherwise, they feared it might lead to unethical practices from some media workers and, as such, deepen the crisis of local journalism. One interviewee, a journalist in her mid-twenties, said that:

> I know that in some local news rooms texts are written by machines, and it bothers me somewhat because I have the impression that it takes away from the seriousness of a profession that is already struggling. Journalists already have a very poor reputation, so when I see that in other newsrooms this is being overused – even partially – it worries me. I am afraid that people simply will not want to return to these media, will not want to read our articles, or even check the news, because they will see them as nothing more than news produced by a robot (Interview PL 3).

Another journalist feared that unregulated usage of platforms, such as ChatGPT would lead to "the lowering of journalists standards in the region" (Interview PL 5).

As it has already been mentioned, the interviewees were optimists in their expectations of local journalism in the age of AI. Moreover, in their opinion the introduction of digital technologies could help them perform their activities better, and consequently, help them serve their communities better. They especially appreciated the ability to a much faster search for information – on condition that humans still control this process:

> I have used it myself to some extent as well, but more as a basis for certain pieces of information. In any case, it still has to pass through a human filter. It is a fairly quick and easy way to search for specific content" (Interview PL 1).

Some doubts concerning AI in local journalism were expressed by the most experienced journalists. One of them, working for a local printed newspaper, said:

> I come from a journalistic generation for whom it was genuinely important to put something of oneself into the work – to show the world through one's own perspective. To offer a vision of the world shaped by my sensitivity and my knowledge, and by the principles I mentioned a moment ago. That vision did not have to appeal to everyone. Today, however, the threats are significant and clearly visible. It is obvious that if something is easier, people will gravitate toward it. It has always been this way: something that makes life easier does not necessarily make it wiser. In this case, within 30 seconds or a bit more, one can suddenly obtain a well-produced piece of information. But it is artificial information – it will always be artificial. Even if it is perfectly written in grammatical and orthographic terms, it will still remain artificial (Interview PL 5).

The interviewees remained optimistic when asked about the future of local journalism in the age of AI. Although they admitted that new technologies drew concerns among fellow journalists, they were far from believing that journalism in its present form is prone to extinction. As one of the interviewees highlighted:

> There were also voices saying things like, "Oh my, artificial intelligence is going to replace journalists – what are we even needed for, if our profession is threatened by the way all this works?" I believe that this is absolutely not the case.

> On the contrary, artificial intelligence can support us and help us simply do our job, making it easier (Interview PL 1).

In the opinion of the interviewees, new technologies could never substitute human journalists, especially at the local level, where it was important to establish direct contact with community members. In addition to this, they indicated the "mechanical" nature of AI and new technologies, as well as their tendency to make simple mistakes and produce uninteresting content. A journalist who works in a local radio station said that:

> I happen to represent a medium that, in my view, is difficult to replace with artificial intelligence. This is because we work with emotions and impressions – we convey emotions and experiences. And that is something AI is not yet capable of doing. Radio, after all, is about feeling; it is about the voice. It is about the presenter's personality and the voices of real people. I cannot accept a situation in which a journalist would, for example, send me audio composed of sounds generated by artificial intelligence. That would be unacceptable (Interview PL 1).

Baden-Württemberg

The content-structuring qualitative content analysis makes it clear that, in local journalism, AI is primarily embedded within existing workflows, where it serves mainly to increase efficiency and streamline standardised processes. At the same time, the interviews show that key journalistic practices – in particular, writing, content evaluation and responsibility for published content – remain strongly protected by professional standards and are not readily delegated to technical systems. AI thus functions less as a replacement and more as a supplementary tool that takes on specific sub-tasks, while key core competencies are deliberately retained by humans.

Use of AI and perception in everyday life

Among the respondents, the use of AI focuses primarily on two key areas of activity: data-intensive research processes and the processing of highly standardised content. In research, AI is used primarily where extensive datasets or a large number of sources need to be reviewed. One data journalist describes how an AI system analysed "around 500 websites" and "almost every single value was correct," thereby highlighting the potential for streamlining time-consuming search and evaluation steps. In his experience, AI can thus take on tasks that previously required considerable time without the results generally losing any reliability. The interviewees also report noticeable efficiency gains when processing repetitive formats – such as news briefs or police reports. One journalist describes how a particular format took "about 15 minutes" to process manually, while the same piece took "around 10 minutes" with AI support. Use is primarily focused on content with a clear structure and a comparatively low level of complexity, where information is presented according to fixed patterns. Here, AI generates initial drafts or pre-structures content, which is then editorially reviewed and adapted.

Beyond these established areas of application, there is evidence of experimental and, in some cases, very far-reaching use of AI, particularly in the freelance sector. One freelance journalist reports that they had set up and simulated "a fully agentic newsroom" which processed content automatically and "automatically published everything." Such scenarios point to attempts to provide technical support for, or partially automate, entire production chains – from research and copywriting to publication. At the same time, human control remains crucial even in these cases; the interviewees emphasise that, ultimately, editorial review or approval must always take place. When it comes to the actual writing of journalistic articles, however, the use of AI remains significantly more limited. Here, the interviewees use AI primarily for support, for example for structuring suggestions, alternative phrasing or immediate feedback on clarity. One interviewee describes the benefit as receiving "feedback instantly," including "suggestions for how you could phrase something." The core activity of text production – in particular, the selection, prioritisation and organisation of information – continues to be viewed by the respondents as a key journalistic skill that should not be outsourced to AI.

Perceptions of AI

Overall, perceptions of AI are ambivalent and characterised by a variety of interpretative frameworks. Some respondents describe AI primarily as a functional tool that performs clearly defined tasks and helps to identify patterns in data or streamline processes. One interviewee describes AI in this context as "a kind of pattern machine," thereby emphasising its role as a technical aid that supports processes but does not make journalistic decisions autonomously. At the same time, there are clearly more critical assessments, particularly with regard to standardised content. One freelance journalist makes the pointed prediction of "the death of average, middle-of-the-road journalism," thereby referring to the expected pressure from automation on those offerings that lack distinctiveness and have a low degree of differentiation. From this perspective, AI appears as a potentially disruptive technology that fundamentally changes certain segments of journalism or even renders them obsolete. At the organisational level, attitudes range from great openness to marked scepticism. The interviews point to newsrooms where "many are excited" about experimenting with new tools, while at the same time "others are hesitant" and place greater weight on risks or uncertainties. This range suggests a process of transformation in which norms, expectations and concrete experiences with AI have not yet stabilised and are still being negotiated.

Impact on journalistic work processes

A key finding of the analysis concerns the perceived effects of AI on work organisation and process logic. In almost all interviews, significant efficiency gains were cited, particularly in research, data processing and text-related preparation. One interviewee summed this up succinctly: "…efficiency obviously increases massively…." The automation of routine tasks creates scope which, in the interviewees' view, can be used for more demanding tasks, such as in-depth research or analytical reporting. These effects are accompanied by a shift in the understanding of the journalist's role. While journalistic work used to be heavily focused on the independent production of content, several interviewees describe a shift towards coordinating and curating activities. One freelancer succinctly sums up this shift: "I used to do everything myself, now I orchestrate it, delegate it, curate it." Journalists increasingly see themselves in the role of process managers who oversee AI-supported workflows, review interim results and carry out the final quality control. The automation of routine tasks is also seen as a relief in day-to-day work. It leads to a reduction in time-consuming, low-creativity tasks, freeing up more capacity for more complex activities such as research discussions, conducting interviews or investigative projects. At the same time, some respondents point out that new tasks are being added – such as configuring systems, checking for potential errors and documenting decisions – meaning that job profiles are shifting overall rather than the workload simply disappearing.

Opportunities offered by the use of AI

The interviews highlight several opportunities associated with the use of AI in local journalism. In addition to the increased efficiency already described, the potential for improving quality is particularly emphasised. Some interviewees stress that AI helps to shift resources away from repetitive tasks towards more content-intensive activities. This makes it possible to achieve "better quality... more depth" and to "actually do deep research," as one person put it. By relieving journalists of routine tasks, they can focus their attention more strongly on the core tasks of the profession – such as investigative research, analytical assessments and locally rooted background reporting. AI is understood here not as a replacement, but as a kind of infrastructure that allows existing resources to be deployed in a more targeted manner. For freelancers in particular, this also opens up new opportunities to develop innovative business models. Through the flexible, experimental use of AI, they can create specialised offerings, such as data-driven formats, automated services for specific client groups, or new hybrid forms combining automated and curated reporting. The high degree of autonomy within this group makes it easier to experiment with new tools and workflows without being constrained by rigid organisational structures.

Risks and challenges

In addition to the opportunities, the analysis identifies a number of risks and challenges which, in the respondents' view, are closely linked to the use of AI. A key point of criticism concerns the risk of a decline in quality due to AI-generated content. One interviewee described how certain AI-generated texts appeared "simply diluted" and had "no real news value." This assessment highlights the tendency for automated content to lead to standardisation, clichéd phrasing and a dumbing down of content if it is not carefully curated. Another significant risk concerns the credibility of journalistic content. Several interviewees point out that, due to hallucinations and erroneous information, AI is capable of producing false or misleading content. One interviewee expressly warned that the technology could point in a "completely wrong direction." This possibility is perceived as a significant challenge to journalistic quality standards and relationships of trust with the audience, as errors in the automated process ultimately fall back on the editorial team responsible. Furthermore, some interviewees express concerns regarding potential impacts on the labour market. Particularly in fields of work with high potential for automation, employees ask themselves, "...will this affect my job?." This uncertainty primarily affects routine, highly standardised job roles, while highly specialised or locally rooted roles are generally considered to be more resilient. These concerns are compounded by perceived uncertainties regarding ethical and data protection issues. Respondents highlight unresolved issues concerning transparency, the traceability of automated decisions, the handling of sensitive data, and the formulation of binding guidelines.

Organisational conditions and future prospects

The findings reveal clear differences in how media organisations approach AI. Larger publishing houses often have specialised structures in place, such as AI hubs, training programmes and guidelines, which strategically steer the use of AI. Smaller editorial teams use AI more selectively, heavily dependent on individual skills and resources. In both contexts, tech-savvy journalists drive integration forward and act as internal advocates. Freelancers occupy a special position: fewer organisational constraints allow for faster, experimental use of tools, but make them more reliant on their own responsibility and networks, as institutional safeguards are lacking. Looking to the future, respondents anticipate a hybrid model in which AI takes on specific tasks, while responsibility for content remains with humans: "...AI can support the process... but humans remain responsible...." Full automation is rejected. Instead, polarisation is predicted: standardised content will be automated to a greater extent, while high-quality journalism will remain human-driven. Particularly in local journalism, those interviewed emphasise the indispensable role of personal contacts and contextual expertise. One respondent sums this up succinctly: "...the more local it gets... the more important your own phone book is...." Local networks and individual knowledge thus form the framework within which AI can be meaningfully integrated.

Discussion

The findings of this comparative study illustrate a moderate to high level of innovation readiness for generative AI in local journalism in both regions, albeit qualified by structural differences, as predicted by Zerfaß's (2005) Innovation Readiness Framework. In Baden-Württemberg, a pragmatic integration of AI as an efficiency tool for routine tasks predominates ("efficiency obviously increases massively"), while West Pomerania displays an optimistic yet resource-constrained attitude: AI is viewed as an accelerator ("much faster search for information"), yet a lack of regulations raises fears of ethical lapses ("texts are written by machines... produced by a robot"). Both regions protect core practices normatively but highlight differing levels of readiness: Baden-Württemberg utilises capacities for experimentation ("fully agentic newsroom"), while West Pomerania emphasises human filters ("still has to pass through a human filter").

A regional comparison of openness to innovation

The explanatory framework gains depth through comparison. At the cultural level, Baden-Württemberg exhibits openness towards AI as a "pattern machine," complemented by a shift in roles towards orchestration ("orchestrate it, delegate it'), which van den Hoed et al. (2022) confirm as a positive climate. In West Pomerania, a generational ambivalence shapes the climate: younger people optimise with AI ("artificial intelligence can support us"), while older people criticise "artificial information" as a loss of personal perspective – a conflict between tradition and innovation, as described by Zammuto and O'Connor (1992). Organisational capacities show greater differentiation: Baden-Württemberg's AI hubs and guidelines promote strategic adoption, while West Pomerania's limited resources force selective use, dependent on individual multipliers. Freelancers in both regions operate autonomously, yet West Pomerania's focus on community service ("work with people") reinforces the rejection of pure automation.

The findings address RQ1 (perception): both groups view AI as a support, not a replacement – in Baden-Württemberg as disruptive to mediocrity ("the death of average journalism'), in West Pomerania as a complement to emotional connection ("radio is about feeling'), which expands on Schapals and Porlezza (2020). RQ2 (Regional Differences) confirms Wallerstein's semi-periphery: West Pomerania's optimism despite scepticism ("AI will not replace us") reflects lower capacities, while Baden-Württemberg's willingness to experiment indicates higher readiness. RQ3 (Factors): Resources, norms and local networks ("your own phone book" vs. "contact with people") modulate readiness, as Cózar et al. (2022) supplement regarding digital competences. Opportunities ("more depth"; "help serve communities better") fit within the framework, but risks – misperceptions ("wrong direction"), credibility, the labour market ("will this affect my job?") – reveal shortcomings: West Pomerania fears damage to its reputation ("lowering of standards"), Baden-Württemberg ethical grey areas. Local resilience dominates: personal contacts make journalism "irreplaceable" ("presenter's personality").

Limitations and Outlook

This study provides exploratory insights into the perception and use of generative AI in local journalism in West Pomerania and Baden-Württemberg. The findings show that journalists predominantly view AI as a supportive tool that contributes in particular to increased efficiency, without, however, replacing the core journalistic skills based on experience, contextual knowledge and social interaction. At the same time, it becomes clear that the introduction of such technologies is viewed with ambivalence: alongside perceived opportunities, uncertainties remain regarding quality standards, credibility and professional norms. However, the significance of the findings is limited by several factors. The comparatively small sample size does not allow for generalisations about the local media systems of the regions studied. Furthermore, this is a snapshot of a dynamically evolving technological environment in which attitudes and usage practices can change rapidly. The focus on two regions, as well as potential distortions arising from translation processes, must also be taken into account when interpreting the results.

Against this backdrop, there is a need for further research. Future studies could employ quantitative methods to include larger sample sizes, thereby systematically capturing the prevalence and determinants of AI use. It also seems advisable to conduct longitudinal studies to analyse changes in perception and actual usage over time. An expanded regional comparison incorporating additional European contexts could also help to provide a more nuanced understanding of structural differences in the approach to AI. Furthermore, future research should place greater emphasis on the audience's perspective, particularly with regard to trust and acceptance of AI-generated content. Similarly, research into training and skills requirements in journalism, as well as the economic impacts of AI use in local newsrooms, would be valuable. Finally, a more in-depth examination of ethical and regulatory frameworks also appears necessary to ensure the responsible use of generative AI in journalistic contexts. Overall, the findings illustrate that the integration of generative artificial intelligence into local journalism should be understood not merely as a technological challenge, but rather as a transformation process embedded within social and organisational contexts. Further research can help to provide a more nuanced understanding of this process and to develop practical guidelines for the use of AI in local media.

Bibliography

Basch, J. M., Melchers, K. G., Kurz, A., Krieger, M., & Miller, L. (2020). "It Takes More Than a Good Camera: Which Factors Contribute to Differences Between Face-to-Face Interviews and Videoconference Interviews Regarding Performance Ratings and Interviewee Perceptions?" *Journal of Business and Psychology*, *36*(5), 921–940. <https://doi.org/10.1007/s10869-020-09714-3>

Belina, A. (2023). "Semi-structured Interviewing as a Tool for Understanding Informal Civil Society". *Voluntary Sector Review*, *14*(2), 331–347. <https://doi.org/10.1332/204080522X16454629995872>.

Borchardt, A. (2025). EBU News Report 2025: Leading newsrooms in the age of generative AI. European Broadcasting Union. https://www.ebu.ch/files/live/sites/ebu/files/Publications/Reports/open/EBU_News_report_2025_Leading%20Newsrooms_AI.pdf

Cózar, S. R. d., Escolar, M. P., & Navazo-Ostúa, P. (2022). "Digital Competencies for New Journalistic Work in Media Outlets: A Systematic Review". *Media and Communication*, *10*(1), 27–42. <https://doi.org/10.17645/mac.v10i1.4439>.

de-Lima-Santos, M., & Ceron, W. (2022). "Artificial Intelligence in News Media: Current Perceptions and Future Outlook". *Journalism and Media*, *3*(1), 13–26. <https://doi.org/10.3390/journalmedia3010002>.

Doody, O., & Noonan, M. (2013). "Preparing and Conducting Interviews to Collect Data". *Nurse Researcher*, *20*(5), 28–32. <https://doi.org/10.7748/nr2013.05.20.5.28.e327>

Dierickx, L., Opdahl, A. L., Khan, S. A., Lindén, C., & Rojas, D. C. G. (2024). "A Data-centric Approach for Ethical and Trustworthy AI in Journalism". *Ethics and Information Technology*, *26*(4). <https://doi.org/10.1007/s10676-024-09801-6>.

Gutiérrez-Caneda, B., Vázquez-Herrero, J., & García, X. L. (2023). "AI Application in Journalism: ChatGPT and the Uses and Risks of an Emergent Technology", *El Profesional De La Información*, *32*(5). <https://doi.org/10.3145/epi.2023.sep.14>.

Gynnild, A. (2013). "Journalism Innovation Leads to Innovation Journalism: The Impact of Computational Exploration on Changing Mindsets". *Journalism*, *15*(6), 713–730. <https://doi.org/10.1177/1464884913486393>.

Hammond, P. (2017). "From Computer-assisted to Data-driven: Journalism and Big Data". *Journalism*, *18*(4), 408–424. <https://doi.org/10.1177/1464884915620205>

Howard, A. B. (2014). The art and science of data-driven journalism. Tow Center for Digital Journalism, Columbia University. https://doi.org/10.7916/D8Q531V1

Kuckartz, U. (2018). Qualitative Inhaltsanalyse. Methoden, Praxis, Computerunterstützung (4. Aufl.). Weinheim: Beltz Juventa.

Lopezosa, Carlos and Codina, Lluís and Pont-Sorribes, Carles and Vállez, Mari, Use of Generative Artificial Intelligence in the Training of Journalists: Challenges, uses and Training Proposal (June 24, 2023). Available at SSRN: https://ssrn.com/abstract=6093486 or http://dx.doi.org/10.2139/ssrn.6093486

Loosen, W., Reimer, J., & De Silva-Schmidt, F. (2020). "Data-driven Reporting: An On-going (R)Evolution? An Analysis of Projects Nominated for the Data Journalism Awards 2013–2016". *Journalism*, *21*(9), 1246–1263.

Luttrell, R., Wallace, A. A., McCollough, C., & Lee, J. (2020). "The Digital Divide: Addressing Artificial Intelligence in Communication Education". *Journalism & Mass Communication Educator*, *75*(4), 470–482. <https://doi.org/10.1177/1077695820925286>.

Mayring, P. (2015). Qualitative Inhaltsanalyse: Grundlagen und Techniken (12. Aufl.). Weinheim: Beltz.

Ndlovu, M. (2024). "Audience Perceptions of AI-driven News Presenters: A Case of "Alice" in Zimbabwe". *Media, Culture & Society*, *46*(8), 1692–1706. <https://doi.org/10.1177/01634437241270982>.

Parasie, S., & Dagiral, E. (2013). "Data-driven Journalism and the Public Good: "Computer-assisted-reporters" and "Programmer-journalists" in Chicago". *New Media & Society*, *15*(6), 853–871.

Peña-Fernández, S., Ayerdi, K. M., Ureta, A. L., & Díaz-Noci, J. (2023). "Without Journalists, There Is No Journalism: The Social Dimension of Generative Artificial Intelligence in the Media", *El Profesional De La Información*, *32*(2). <https://doi.org/10.3145/epi.2023.mar.27>.

Ruiz, M. J. U., Verdú, F. J. M., & López, J. M. T. (2023). "Use of Artificial Intelligence in Synthetic Media: First Newsrooms Without Journalists",

El Profesional De La Información, *32*(2). <https://doi.org/10.3145/epi.2023.mar.03>.

Salazar, G., & Russi-Vigoya, M. N. (2021). "Technology Readiness Level as the Foundation of Human Readiness Level". *Ergonomics in Design*, *29*(4), 25–29.

Schapals, A. K. & Porlezza, C. (2020). "Assistance or Resistance? Evaluating the Intersection of Automated Journalism and Journalistic Role Conceptions". *Media and Communication*, *8*(3), 16–26. <https://doi.org/10.17645/mac.v8i3.3054>.

Simon, F. M., Nielsen, R. K., & Fletcher, R. (2025). "Generative AI and News Report 2025: How People Think about AI's Role in Journalism and Society". *Reuters Institute for the Study of Journalism*. <https://doi.org/10.60625/risj-5bjv-yt69>.

van den Hoed, M. W., Backhaus, R., de Vries, E., Hamers, J. P., & Daniëls, R. (2022). "Factors Contributing to Innovation Readiness in Health Care Organizations: A Scoping Review". *BMC Health Services Research*, *22*(1), 997.

Webster, A., & Gardner, J. (2019). "Aligning Technology and Institutional Readiness: The Adoption of Innovation". *Technology Analysis & Strategic Management*, *31*(10), 1229–1241.

Wenger, D., Hossain, M. S., & Senseman, J. R. (2024). "AI and the Impact on Journalism Education". *Journalism & Mass Communication Educator*, *80*(1), 97–114. <https://doi.org/10.1177/10776958241296497>.

Zammuto, R. F., & O'Connor, E. J. (1992). "Gaining Advanced Manufacturing Technologies' Benefits: The Roles of Organization Design and Culture". *Academy of Management Review*, *17*(4), 701–728. <https://doi.org/10.5465/amr.1992.4279062>.

Zerfaß, A. (2005). "Innovation Readiness". *Innovation Journalism*, *2*(8), 1–27.

Industry 5.0 and human-centric workplaces

Brice Miard[1], *Maxime Daniel*[1], *Nadine Couture*[1]

ABSTRACT
This paper explores the opportunities and challenges of Industry 5.0, with a specific focus on human-centric workplaces. The aim is to bridge the gap between technological advancement and human welfare. A key aspect in manufacturing is understanding material mechanics. While simulation software is essential, its virtualisation can limit workers' grasp of mechanical properties. By providing new kind of human-machine interfaces, such as tangible interfaces, it is possible to exploit both the cognitive substrate and the kinaesthetic capacities of workers more effectively. Tangible interfaces link digital data, processed by computers, to physical elements that users can manipulate.

This study examines the cognitive processes involved in such interactions. We conducted an experiment using a software for the computing of the strength of materials and a tangible interface, where participants manipulated a virtual beam. Results show that multisensory tangible interfaces enhance immersion and understanding compared to traditional graphical interfaces. The multimodal characteristics allow for better cognitive resource distribution, leading to improved performance and reduced mental fatigue.

Harnessing human-machine collaboration through tangible interfaces fosters confidence, deeper understanding, and overall well-being for Industry 5.0 workers.

Keywords: Ubiquitous computing, tangible interaction, cognitive load, future of work, mechanics of materials

Introduction

Ubiquitous computing represents a key evolution for Industry 5.0, by seamlessly integrating technology into the everyday environment to enhance efficiency, human-machine collaboration, and user experience. Industry 5.0 complements the existing Industry 4.0 paradigm by highlighting research and innovation as drivers for a transition to a sustainable, human-centric and resilient European industry. It moves focus from shareholder to stakeholder value, with benefits for all concerned. Industry 5.0 attempts to capture the value of new technologies, providing prosperity beyond jobs and growth, while respecting planetary boundaries, and placing the well-being of the industry worker at the centre of the production process Industry 5.0.

---

1 Univ. Bordeaux, ESTIA-Institute of Technology, EstiaR, F-64210 Bidart, France2Hager Controls, F-33600 Pessac, France
Corresponding author Email: n.couture@estia.fr

This paper will explore the opportunities and challenges of future of work in Industry 5.0, with a specific focus on human-centric workplaces. The aim is to bridge the gap between technological advancement and human welfare. A key aspect in manufacturing is understanding material mechanics. While simulation software is essential, its virtualisation can limit workers' grasp of mechanical properties. By providing new kinds of human-machine interfaces, such as tangible interfaces, it is possible to exploit together and better, the cognitive substrate and the kinaesthetic capacities of the workers in future work. In this paper, we use the term "cognitive substrate" to refer to all the underlying structures and processes that enable cognition, i.e. the ability to perceive, understand, learn and reason. The concept of cognitive substrate is essential for designing interfaces adapted to users' cognitive abilities and limitations. Tangible interfaces link digital data, processed by computers, to physical elements that users can manipulate.

A study was conducted using a software for the computing of the strength of materials and a tangible interface, where participants manipulated a real beam that controlled the virtual beam (very simple digital twin). This prototype used part of the hardware developed in nawel. Results showed that multisensory tangible interfaces enhance immersion and understanding compared to traditional graphical interfaces. The multimodal characteristics allow for better cognitive resource distribution, leading to improved performance and reduced mental fatigue. Harnessing human-machine collaboration through tangible interfaces fosters confidence, deeper understanding, and overall well-being for Industry 5.0 workers.

In the following, we will detail the experimental protocol employed, present key results obtained from comparing graphical user interface (GUI) and a tangible user interface (TUI) approaches, and provide specific recommendations for future TUI research and development in the field of material mechanics.

Case presentation

Our case study, detailed below, is centred around the comparative analysis of two types of human-machine interfaces: a traditional graphical user interface and a tangible user interface, in the specific context of learning and understanding material mechanics.

This study examines the use of TUI to enhance understanding of material mechanics, crucial in human-centric Industry 5.0. Traditional simulation software's virtualisation can hinder comprehension. A within-subjects experiment was conducted using RDM6 software, with participants manipulating a virtual beam via both a GUI and a TUI. RDM is a software package for teaching structural design using the finite element method.

The TUI aimed to reduce cognitive load and improve immersion, offering a more intuitive grasp of mechanical properties.

The main objective is then to evaluate whether a tangible interface improves the acquisition of knowledge and the understanding of mechanical concepts, performance, and cognitive load, compared to a traditional interface.

Hypothesis. We have put forward four hypotheses:

- (H1) Subjects manipulate the virtual beam more easily with the tangible interface and complete the exercises more easily with the TUI than with the GUI.
- (H2) The use of a tangible interface improves understanding of the task as opposed to formal learning.
- (H3) The tangible interface requires less cognitive load and therefore less cognitive fatigue than with a conventional interface.
- (H4) The tangible interfaces equalise spatial representation abilities regardless of gender.

Participants. 20 volunteers, as many men as women, with no prior experience in material mechanics, in the use of RDM6 simulation software or equivalent software. The subjects were aged between 22 and 26, all right-handed. They were not pregnant and had no neurological, psychological or physical disorders. The participants were divided into two groups.

Experimental protocol. Participants performed basic exercises on the material resistance software RDM6, using both the GUI and the TUI interface. The first group started with the GUI interface, while the second started with the TUI interface.

The exercises consisted of beam deformation tasks

A questionnaire was administered at the end of the test to collect the subjects' impressions.

Exercises. Each participant had to do four exercises. They were all designed in the same way. We present one below.

a) Create a beam with the following parameters:
   - Material: Steel
   - Section: Solid circular type (cylinder), Diameter d=0.1 m, Length: L=10 m
b) At the right-hand end, apply a vertical downward force.
   Q1: For what value of force has the beam with the solid section passed into the plastic range?
c) Create a second beam with the same parameters as above, changing the type of section to hollow circular (tube).
d) For the right-hand end, apply a vertical downward force.
   Q2: For what value of force did the beam with the hollow section enter the plastic domain?
   Q3: Which of the two beams enters the plastic domain first? Choose one from the following 2:
   - The solid section beam.
   - The hollow section beam.
   Q4: Why? Choose one of the following three answers:
   - There is a problem with the simulation because it is illogical.
   - The weight of the profile in the solid section leads to inherent bending, which accentuates the deformation and therefore the failure. deformation and therefore failure.
   - A hollow section is more rigid than a solid section.

Measures. Quantitative, qualitative and physiological measures are collected. The two quantitative measures are time required to perform each exercise and number of errors. Qualitative measures are the types of errors and subjective impressions via a questionnaire. The physiological measures recorded were heart rate and electrodermal response, in order to assess stress levels. Electrodermal response was measured with ProComp Infiniti model SA7500 and heart rate with Geonaute. The subjects were filmed during their and all the data was synchronised with The Observer software. The aim of these measurements is to assess the stress levels of the individuals.

The tangible interface is composed of a ShapeTape (Measurand product) ShapeTape that captures physical deformations of the ribbon and transmits the movements to the computer (see figure fig:ShapeTape). An envelope to the ShapeTape, composed of a flexible boiler tube and a tensioning system, allows adjusting the physical (elastic) characteristics of the beam according to its size, section, and weight.

Results and discussion

Results. Our analysis of the two interfaces (TUI and GUI) considered four parameters: the time to complete the exercises, the accuracy of the results, the gender of the subjects, cognitive fatigue, and stress.

Subjects completed the exercises more quickly with the tangible interface than with the mouse-keyboard interface, averaging 90 seconds less with the tangible interface

The tangible interface allows non-expert users to better evaluate the value of forces exerted on the beam. This difference in time is important for reducing the mental fatigue of the subject during longer and more complex tasks. Performance comparison with the analysis of the quality of answers: validation of hypothesis 2 concerning understanding of the task.

Hypothesis 3 concerning cognitive load was not validated by physiological measurements, as we did not observe any significant variation in heart rate.

The results do not depend on the gender of the subjects. Tangible interfaces allow for a linearisation of abilities, even though a small but significant male advantage in visual-spatial working memory exists, with age and specific tasks modulating the effects. Hypothesis 4 was not validated. Qualitatively, the subjects preferred to work with the tangible.

Discussion. The Tangible interfaces enhance immersion and understanding compared to traditional graphical interfaces. Moreover, the multimodal characteristics allow for better cognitive resource distribution, leading to improved performance and reduced mental fatigue. Despite these very positive conclusions, our study revealed several limitations, which could be overcome in future research.

First, the tensioner that adjusts the elasticity of our "beam" was experienced differently depending on the individual.

Second, there were synchronisation problems between the ShapeTape and the RDM6 software, which regularly caused bugs. The RDM6 software is static; subjects indicated that it would be more pleasant and easier to use if the twisting of the beam occurred simultaneously on the software and on the tangible part.

Third, the recorded physiological measurements (electrodermal response and heart rate) did not show significant differences between the two interfaces. This may be because the exercises are too easy to generate stress and that the interface does not optimise working memory. In a second stage, we will perform more complex exercises.

Fourth, subjects did not feel the elastic limit of the beam before it passed into the plastic domain. This tangible interface offers purely passive haptic feedback. We could design and fabricate a new prototype with a dynamic haptic feedback system.

Conclusions and recommendations

We have conducted a within-subjects experiment to find that tangible interfaces are more suitable to perform mechanics of materials tasks compared to classic graphical interfaces.

Participants (N = 20) performed beam deformation tasks in RDM6, using GUI and TUI. The TUI aimed to improve mechanical property understanding. Time, accuracy, and subjective feedback were recorded. Order was counterbalanced to mitigate learning effects. Physiological measures (heart rate, electrodermal response) were collected.

TUI significantly reduced task completion time (90 s faster, $p < 0.05$). With the tangible interface, the subjects registered 71.

The multimodal nature of TUIs, providing both visual and haptic feedback, appears to enhance cognitive processing and reduce cognitive load. No significant gender effect was observed. Physiological data showed no clear differences.

In conclusion, TUIs offer promising advantages for learning material mechanics, particularly for novices, by reducing task time and improving comprehension.

In perspective, we recommend, on the technological plan, to address the issues with the tensioner mechanism to ensure a more consistent and user-friendly experience across different strength levels and to incorporate active haptic feedback. Indeed, enhance the TUI with active haptic feedback allows users to feel the elastic limit of the material and the transition into the plastic domain. This could involve integrating devices like the Phantom (from 3D Systems company) to provide force feedback or going towards shape-changing tangible interfaces, such as linebase.

With regards to measures, it could be interesting to conduct more extensive physiological measurements, potentially including electroencephalography (EEG), to gain a deeper understanding of cognitive load and stress levels associated with each interface.

Finally, for Industry 5.0 future work, the integration of tangible interfaces to exploit workers' cognitive and kinaesthetic abilities holds great promise to bridging the gap between technological advancement and human well-being.

Acknowledgements

NotebookLM, based on Google Gemini 2.0 AI, was utilised to generate paragraphs of this text from documents produced exclusively by the authors of this article as part of this research project. The authors would also like to thank Nawel Takouachet for discussions on this subject.

Study on the influence of repeated use of PA12 powder on the evolution of mechanical properties, morphology, and dimensional stability of parts produced using SLS technology

Sebastian Banucha[1], *Tomasz Królikowski*[1], *Sebastian Pecolt*[1], *Andrzej Błażejewski*[1], *Piotr Zmuda Trzebiatowski*[2], *Rafał Wątor*[2]

ABSTRACT

Selective Laser Sintering (SLS) technology generates significant amounts of unsintered polymer powder, the recycling of which is crucial for the economic viability of the process. However, this material (commonly PA12) is subjected to long-term exposure to high temperatures in the build chamber, which leads to its thermal degradation and can negatively affect the properties of the finished parts. This paper presents the results of a study evaluating the impact of tenfold, 100 % recycling of PA12 powder (without adding fresh material) on its properties. As part of the methodology, ten printing cycles were carried out, producing ten standardised samples in each (100 in total). The tests were conducted using a Sintratec Kit printer and a Zwick Z010 TN testing machine. Non-linear degradation of key mechanical properties was observed. Tensile strength (UTS) dropped from 55.13 MPa (Cycle 1) to 24.40 MPa (Cycle 10), representing a loss of 55.7 % of the original strength. In parallel, a clear decrease in elongation at break was found (from 108.95 % to 103.03 %), indicating an increase in the brittleness of the material. Scanning Electron Microscopy (SEM) analysis revealed significant morphological changes in the powder after 10 cycles, including grain agglomeration. A significant decrease in the dimensional stability (shrinkage) of the parts was also noted, where the cross-sectional area of the samples decreased by 10.57 %. Based on the obtained results, a safe PA12 powder recycling "window" of up to four cycles was identified, in which the material retains approximately 90 % of its original tensile strength. Further reuse of the powder without refreshing leads to a rapid decline in mechanical properties and a loss of process repeatability, as illustrated by the increase in the standard deviation of the results. Work on SLS PA12 has been carried out in various aspects for several years (Alejandro et al., 2023; Chao et al., 2021; Dadbakhsh et al., 2017; Damanhuri et al., 2019; Gomes et al., 2022; Jana et al., 2024; Kohutiar et al., 2025; Kumar, 2003; Mielicki et al., 2014; Omar et al., 2022; Prakhyat et al., 2022; Wudy et al. 2014).

Keywords: 3D Printing, Selective Laser Sintering (SLS), PA12, powder recycling, powder reuse, tensile strength, material degradation, thermal ageing, SEM analysis

1 Department of Mechatronics and Automation, Koszalin University of Technology

2 3D Printing Center, Faculty of Mechanical Engineering, Koszalin University of Technology, Śniadeckich 2, 75–453 Koszalin, Poland

Introduction

The modern battlefield and dynamically developing industrial monitoring sectors are increasingly abandoning expensive, reusable platforms in favour of "one-way" solutions – so-called disposable drones. In this new reality, where key parameters become rapid project adaptation, low implementation cost, and reliability during that single, decisive mission, traditional production methods, such as injection moulding, often prove too rigid and time-consuming (Agarwal et al., 2021; Andries & Zaharia, 2025; Kantaros et al., 2025; Kateb et al., 2025; Malik, 2025; MohamedZain et al., 2022; Šostakait et al., 2024). The development of Selective Laser Sintering (SLS) technology and the optimisation of polymer recycling processes constitute key elements of the transformation of Polish enterprises towards the assumptions of Industry 4.0 (Dyczkowska et al., 2023; Koren, 2010; Kostrzewski et al., 2022; Królikowski et al., 2021; Machała et al., 2023; Tomasz et al., 2021; Zahra et al., 2026). The necessity to optimise material consumption in additive technologies does not result solely from economic premises but is also an element of broader reverse logistics strategies and rapid response to broken supply chains, which was observed, among others, during crisis periods (Królikowski et al., 2021; Machała et al., 2023). Optimisation of the material recycling process fits into the broader trend of Logistics 4.0, where Decision-Support Systems (DSS) allowing for effective resource management in the supply chain play a key role (Dyczkowska, Chamier-Gliszczyński et al., 2023; Dyczkowska, Olkiewicz et al., 2023; Dyczkowska et al., 2025; Grunt et al., 2022; Koren, 2010; Kostrzewski et al., 2022; Królikowski et al., 2020; Machała et al., 2022; Tomasz et al., 2021; Zahra et al., 2026).

SLS PA12 powder (Nylon 12) offers a rare compromise: it allows to produce elements with high strength and impact resistance, which simultaneously retain the flexibility necessary to survive launch overloads or difficult weather conditions. Unlike popular home technologies (like FDM), elements made of PA12 powder are characterised by isotropy – they are almost equally strong in every direction, which is critical for aviation structures subjected to complex stresses. Furthermore, SLS technology eliminates the need for support structures, opening new design possibilities for engineers. This enables the creation of complex geometries – from openwork, ultra-light load-bearing structures to integrated ventilation channels – the execution of which using other manufacturing methods would be technically impossible or economically unjustified. This article presents how SLS PA12 powder revolutionises the approach to designing disposable drone structures through an analysis of its physical properties and economic benefits in low-volume production.

Additive Manufacturing (AM) technologies, commonly referred to as 3D printing (Attaran, 2017; Glowinski et al., 2025; Kruth et al., 1998; Zmuda, 2025), are significantly changing contemporary industrial processes, evolving from applications in Rapid Prototyping (RP) to low-volume production of functional end-use parts (Rapid Manufacturing, RM). Among AM methods, Selective Laser Sintering (SLS) occupies a special place, enabling the production of geometrically complex components from thermoplastic polymers without the need for dedicated support structures. During the operation of SLS systems, especially under conditions of repeated use of the same powder bed, a critical aspect remains the control of nanoparticle and volatile organic compound (VOC) emissions, which may arise because of the thermal degradation of polyamide (Królikowski, 2019).

A key barrier to the widespread implementation of SLS technology remains the high cost of consumables, in particular polymer powders such as the commonly used Polyamide 12 (PA12). In a typical printing cycle, most of the material placed in the build chamber is not sintered by the laser beam but acts as a natural support for the produced parts. This results in the generation of a large amount of unsintered powder, the reuse (recycling) of which is standard industrial practice aimed at reducing costs and improving the sustainable nature of production (Zmuda et al., 2025).

However, this practice raises a fundamental engineering challenge. Unsintered powder is not a thermally inert material. Throughout the duration of the printing process, often lasting many hours, the entire volume of the powder bed is maintained at an elevated temperature, close to the melting point of the polymer. This cyclic thermal exposure leads to irreversible material degradation, known as thermal ageing, even if the powder has not been directly subjected to laser action.

Literature studies to date confirm that thermal ageing of PA12 affects its rheological properties (viscosity), degree of crystallinity, and particle morphology. These changes can directly translate into the quality of interlayer bonding, porosity, and final mechanical properties of the finished parts. In industry, various "refreshing" strategies (refresh ratio) are used, consisting of mixing used powder with fresh powder to compensate for this effect. However, there is a lack of detailed, long-term studies on the effects of a 100 % recycling strategy (0 % refresh rate), which, although most economically desirable, carries the greatest risk of degradation.

The aim of this work is a quantitative assessment of the impact of the number of cycles (from 1 to 10) of 100 % reuse of PA12 powder on:

- The evolution of key mechanical properties: tensile strength (UTS), yield strength, modulus of elasticity, and elongation at break.
- Changes in powder morphology, analysed using Scanning Electron Microscopy (SEM).
- Dimensional stability and shrinkage of finished parts.

The ultimate goal of the study is to define the practical limits of safe and efficient PA12 recycling, providing data necessary for cost optimisation of the SLS process in engineering applications.

Materials and research methodology

Research material

Commercial Polyamide 12 (PA12) powder from Sintratec, dedicated to SLS printers of this manufacturer, was used in the research. PA12 is a material commonly used in functional prototyping due to the good balance between strength, flexibility, and chemical resistance. The analysis of non-linear degradation of key mechanical properties of PA12 parts correlates with the results of earlier studies on the thermo-mechanical stability of additively manufactured elements (Królikowski et al., 2019). The material properties declared by the manufacturer, constituting a reference point for the obtained results, are presented in Table 1.

Table 1: Specification of PA12 material (Sintratec) used for testing

Property	Value
Tensile Strength (max load)	51 MPa
Tensile modulus	1.95 GPa
Elongation @ Break	11 %

Hardware platform

Experimental studies were conducted using the following apparatus:

- 3D Printing System: Samples were produced on a desktop SLS printer, Sintratec Kit (Figure 1) (Sintratec AG, Switzerland). The use of low-budget, yet precise systems like the Sintratec Kit allows for the broad implementation of SLS technology not only in industry but also in advanced research and educational processes, which fosters the building of technical competencies of future engineering staff (Królikowski & Mikulski, 2024). The device is equipped with a 2.3 W diode laser. Printing process parameters were controlled using dedicated software, Sintratec Central.
- Testing System: Static tensile tests were carried out on a universal testing machine, Zwick Z010 TN (ZwickRoell GmbH & Co. KG, Germany), equipped with a force sensor with a range of up to 10 kN.
- Auxiliary Systems: A laboratory vibratory sieve was used to recover and homogenise the powder after each printing cycle.

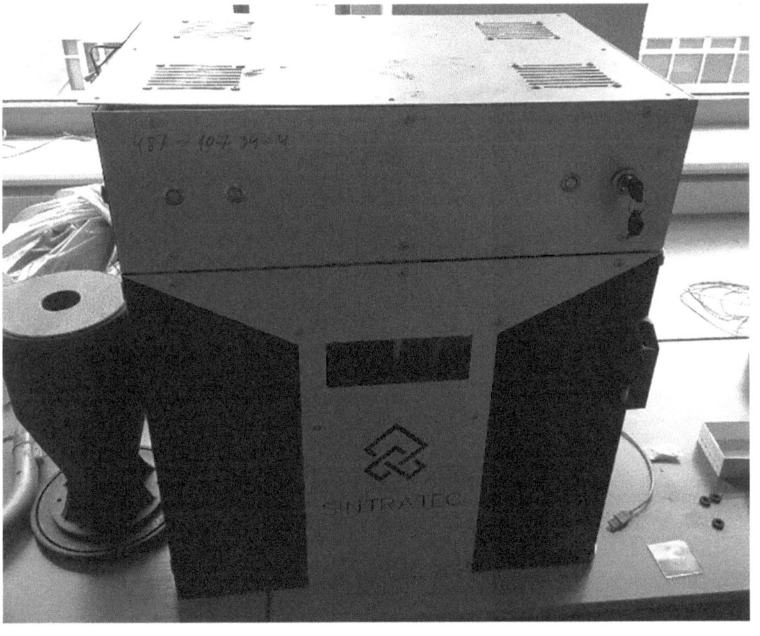

Figure 1: Sintratec Kit SLS printer used in the research.

Sample design and preparation

Samples for mechanical testing (so-called "dog bone") were designed in Solidworks software (Figure 3) in strict accordance with the guidelines of the PN-EN ISO 527-2 standard, as type 1BA samples. This geometry is standard for determining the tensile properties of plastics. The technical drawing of the sample is presented in Figure 2.

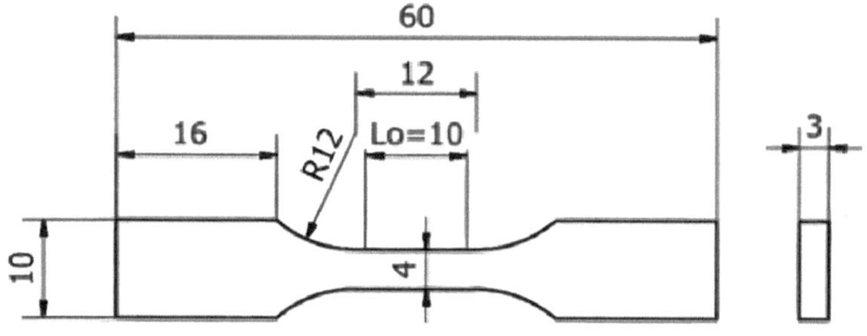

Figure 2: Technical drawing of the test sample compliant with PN-EN ISO 527-2.

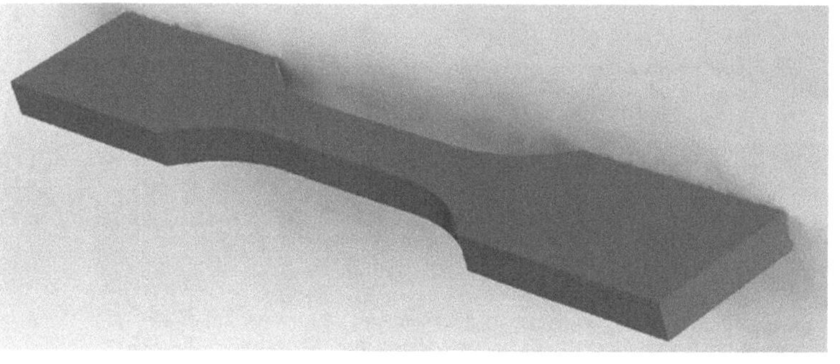

Figure 3: CAD visualisation of the test sample.

Experimental procedure (10-cycle methodology)

The study was based on a rigorous 10-printing-cycle procedure aimed at simulating intensive material ageing under 100 % recycling conditions.

- Step 1 (Cycle 1): The build chamber of the Sintratec Kit printer was filled with 100 % fresh, unused PA12 powder. The first series of ten test samples was printed.

- Step 2 (Recovery): After the printing process was completed and the chamber had completely cooled (which is crucial for stabilising the crystal structure), the printed samples were removed. All remaining unsintered powder ("cake") was collected from the build chamber.
- Step 3 (Sieving): The collected powder was subjected to a sieving process on a vibratory sieve (Figure 4). The aim of this step was to remove any larger agglomerates or partially sintered fragments that could disrupt the subsequent printing process.
- Step 4 (Cycle N+1): The machine's chamber was refilled exclusively with the sieved powder recovered from the previous cycle (Cycle N). A key methodological assumption was the non-use of any refreshing material (so-called 100 % reuse rate / 0 % refresh rate).
- Step 5 (Repetition): Steps 2–4 were systematically repeated until ten full printing cycles were achieved. From each cycle (series), 10 samples were taken for mechanical testing, yielding a total of 100 samples.

Figure 4: Vibratory sieve used for powder recovery after each cycle.

Analysis methodology

- Mechanical Analysis: The static tensile test was conducted in accordance with the PN-EN ISO 527-2 standard on the Zwick Z010 TN machine (Figure 5). Samples were clamped in the machine jaws and stretched at a constant crosshead speed of 1 mm/min (value established in the thesis methodology). Force (N) was recorded as a function of displacement (mm) to calculate: stress (MPa), yield strength (MPa), ultimate tensile strength (UTS, MPa), modulus of elasticity (GPa), and elongation at break (%).

- Morphological Analysis: Powder samples (taken from the fresh batch from Cycle 1 and the 10-times used batch from Cycle 10) were prepared and analysed using Scanning Electron Microscopy (SEM). The examination was performed at an accelerating voltage of 10 kV and working magnifications in the range of 1000x–2000x.
- Dimensional Analysis: Before the tensile test, each of the 100 samples was measured using a calliper to precisely determine the actual cross-sectional area in the gauge length. These data were necessary for the accurate calculation of stress values.

Figure 5: Type 1BA sample (PA12) clamped in the jaws of the Zwick Z010 TN testing machine during the static tensile test.

Structural changes observed in Scanning Electron Microscopy (SEM) in recycled PA12 powder directly translate into inaccuracies in reproducing the internal geometry of details, which is particularly important when designing complex structures with metamaterial features and drone part constructions (Królikowski et al., 2019).

Results and discussion

Influence of recycling cycles on mechanical properties

Key mechanical test results for 100 samples from ten series were collected and averaged for each cycle. Table 2 presents a synthetic summary of the evolution of key mechanical parameters as a function of the number of recycling cycles.

Table 2: Summary results of mechanical properties of PA12 samples in ten recycling cycles

Cycle No. (Series)	Avg. Yield Strength [MPa]	Avg. UTS [MPa]	Avg. Elastic Modulus [GPa]	Avg. Elongation at Break [%]	UTS Std. Dev [MPa]
1	27.51	55.13	1.65	108.95	1.13
2	28.27	51.35	1.6	107.08	1.88
3	29.29	49.74	1.58	106.75	0.73
4	28.9	49.16	1.57	106.62	1.76
5	31.74	47.34	1.55	105.04	2.03
6	30.05	44.98	1.48	104.94	2.09
7	29.45	42.43	1.42	104.58	1.47
8	29.17	37.3	1.29	104.23	3.61
9	27.51	33.16	1.17	103.96	4.15
10	23.91	24.4	1.41	103.03	3.05

Discussion – ultimate tensile strength (UTS)

Analysis of maximum tensile strength (UTS) as a function of recycling cycles (Figure 6) shows a clear, non-linear downward trend. The degradation of properties is not uniform, and three distinct phases can be distinguished:

- Phase 1 (Initial Shock, Cycles 1–2): The first reuse of the powder causes a significant drop in strength by 6.8 %, from 55.13 MPa to 51.35 MPa. This is likely the effect of the first, intense thermal exposure of the entire bed.
- Phase 2 (Stability Plateau, Cycles 2–4): Material properties stabilise. The drop in strength between cycles 2 and 4 is relatively small (from 51.35 MPa to 49.16 MPa). In cycle 4, the material retains 89.2 % of its original strength, which aligns with the thesis conclusion regarding a 90 % threshold.
- Phase 3 (Catastrophic Degradation, Cycles 5–10): After the fifth cycle, a rapid collapse of mechanical properties occurs. The drop between cycles 4 and 10 is drastic (from 49.16 MPa to 24.40 MPa). Ultimately, after 10 cycles, the material loses 55.7 % of its initial strength.

For engineering applications requiring reliability, four cycles of 100 % recycling seem to constitute the limit of acceptability. For printing disposable parts for combat drones, this can be increased to six for testing purposes.

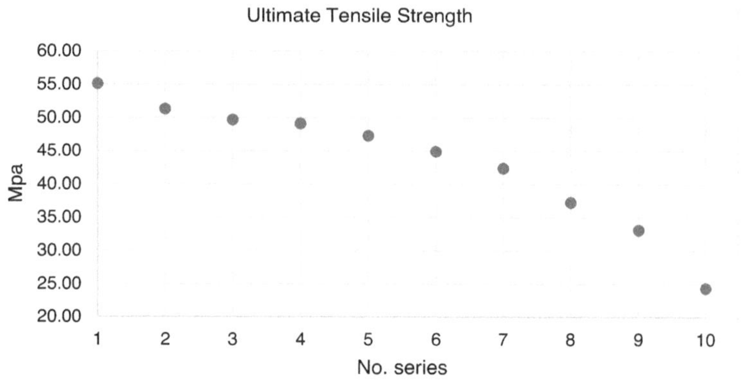

Figure 6: Change in average tensile strength (UTS) over ten recycling cycles.

Discussion – Brittleness and Stiffness

Data concerning elongation at break (Figure 7) and yield strength (Figure 8) reveal a complex mechanism of material ageing. The systematic decrease in elongation at break, from 108.95 % (Cycle 1) to 103.03 % (Cycle 10), is a clear indicator of increased polymer brittleness (embrittlement). The material loses its ability to undergo plastic deformation.

At the same time, data regarding yield strength show a seemingly contradictory trend. This parameter does not decrease but increases in cycles 2–8, reaching a maximum in the fifth cycle (31.74 MPa), a value significantly higher than for fresh powder (27.51 MPa). However, this is not a desirable increase in "useful" strength. It is a classic symptom of polymer degradation. Cyclic heating in the chamber likely causes changes in the crystalline structure of the material (e.g. post-crystallisation), which increases its stiffness and hardness, raising the yield point. This happens, however, at the cost of a drastic drop in ductility. Only after exceeding the critical point of polymer chain degradation (after cycle 8) does the entire structure collapse, and all parameters, including yield strength, fall sharply.

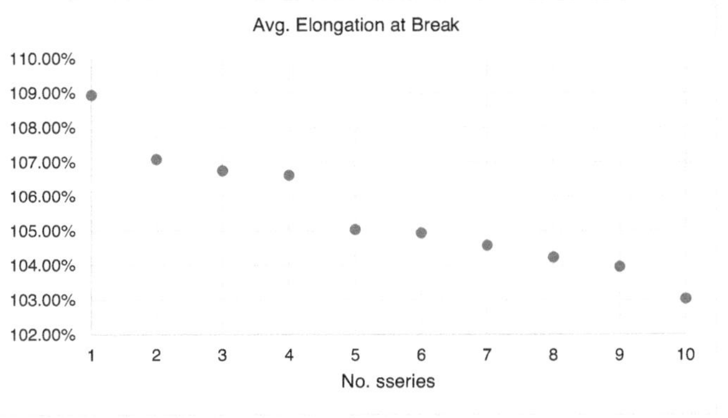

Figure 7: Change in average elongation at break over ten recycling cycles.

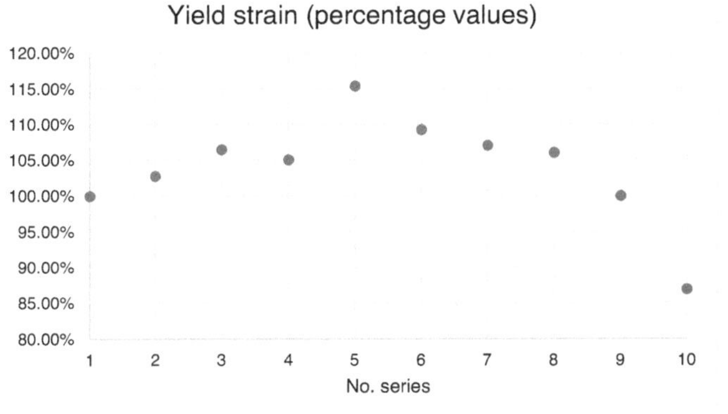

Figure 8: Change in average yield strength over ten recycling cycles.

Discussion – Reliability and Process Repeatability

From an industrial perspective, perhaps the most alarming result is not the drop in average UTS value itself, but the drastic increase in process unpredictability. As shown in Figure 9, the standard deviation for UTS results grows with the number of cycles, reaching a maximum in the ninth cycle (4.15 MPa). In Cycle 1, with an average of 55.13 MPa and a deviation of 1.13 MPa, the process is highly repeatable. However, in Cycle 9, with an average of 33.16 MPa and a deviation of 4.15 MPa, the results become chaotic. This means that statistically, a significant portion of samples (approx. 16 %) may have strength below 29 MPa (one sigma below the mean). Such process instability disqualifies the material after 7–8 recycling cycles from any engineering applications requiring guaranteed reliability.

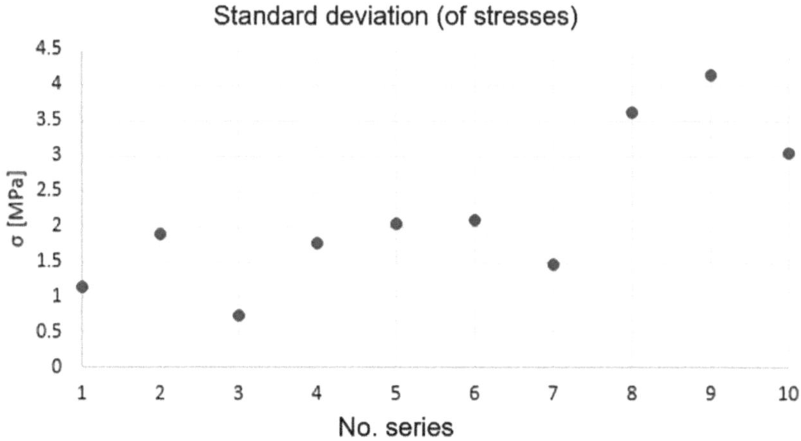

Figure 9: Change in standard deviation of stresses (UTS) over ten recycling cycles.

Impact of recycling on powder morphology and dimensional stability

To understand the physical causes of the observed mechanical degradation, an analysis of powder morphology and a dimensional analysis of finished samples were conducted.

SEM analysis results

Comparison of SEM micrographs of fresh powder (Cycle 1) with 10-times used powder (Cycle 10) reveals fundamental changes in its structure (Figure 10).

Fresh powder consists of relatively smooth, separate grains. Powder from Cycle 10 shows visible degradation of the grain surface, which becomes more porous. A key observation is the phenomenon of agglomeration – "more and more clusters of grains connected to each other" appear. Particles, subjected to repeated heating, begin to partially melt on the surfaces and stick together, forming larger, irregular agglomerates.

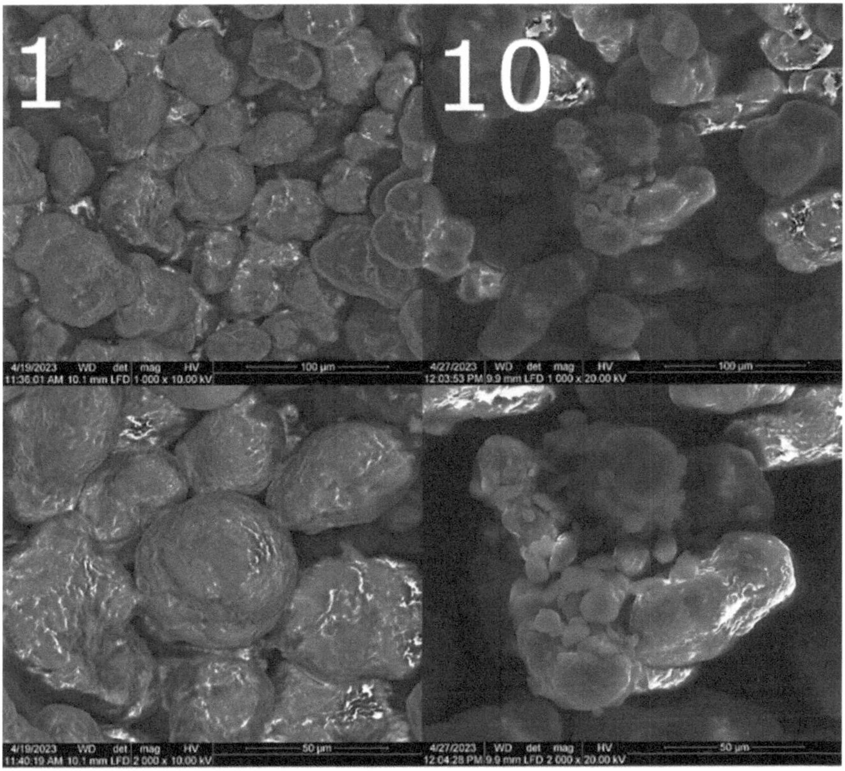

Figure 10: Comparison of SEM images: (left) fresh PA12 powder (Cycle 1), (right) PA12 powder after ten recycling cycles (Cycle 10). Visible surface degradation and grain agglomeration.

Dimensional analysis results

Dimensional analysis of 100 samples showed a systematic loss of dimensional stability. As shown in Figure 11, the actual cross-sectional area of the samples decreases with each subsequent cycle. Ultimately, the cross-sectional area of samples from Cycle 10 was on average 10.57 % smaller than that of samples from Cycle 1. This indicates significant and increasing material shrinkage as it degrades.

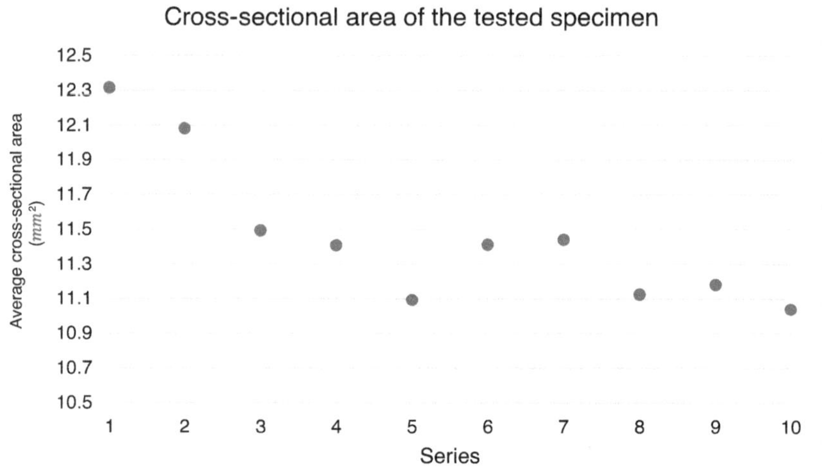

Figure 11: Change (decrease) in the average cross-sectional area of samples over ten recycling cycles, indicating increasing material shrinkage.

Discussion (unified theory of degradation)

The observed mechanical changes (Section 3.1) are a direct result of physical changes in the powder (Section 3.2). The following cause-and-effect chain can be formulated:

1. Long-term, cyclic thermal exposure of the powder in the build chamber (Cause).
2. This leads to partial melting of grain surfaces and the formation of permanent agglomerates (SEM Effect, Figure 10).
3. Agglomeration drastically worsens the rheological properties of the powder, in particular its "flowability".
4. Worsened flowability prevents the printer mechanism (roller) from evenly spreading a thin layer of powder on the build platform.
5. Uneven powder distribution leads to two simultaneous problems:
   o A) Increase in porosity inside the finished detail: Particles are not densely packed before sintering, resulting in more voids in the final structure. Smaller effective load-bearing area directly causes a drastic

drop in UTS (Figure 6) and increased unpredictability of results (Figure 9).

- o B) Change in thermal properties of the powder bed: Different powder packing density changes its local thermal conductivity. This causes disturbances in the sintering process, insufficient or excessive melting, and consequently uncontrolled, increasing material shrinkage (Dimensional Effect, Figure 11).

Powder degradation thus hits the process doubly: it lowers mechanical properties and dimensional accuracy. In precision applications (e.g. fitted parts, snaps), the part may become useless due to unacceptable shrinkage before its strength falls below a critical level.

Conclusions

The study confirmed that repeated (10-fold) reuse of PA12 powder in SLS technology, with no refreshing with fresh material (0 % refresh rate), leads to significant, non-linear degradation of mechanical properties, a decrease in process repeatability, and a loss of dimensional stability of finished parts.

The key findings of the study are as follows:

- Drop in strength: Tensile strength (UTS) dropped by 55.7 % after 10 cycles, from an initial value of 55.13 MPa (Cycle 1) to 24.40 MPa (Cycle 10).
- Increase in brittleness: The material exhibits progressive brittleness, confirmed by a systematic decrease in elongation at break (from 108.95 % to 103.03 %).
- Loss of repeatability: The process becomes highly unpredictable after approx. 7 cycles. The standard deviation of UTS results increased from 1.13 MPa (Cycle 1) to 4.15 MPa (Cycle 9), making the material unsuitable for engineering applications requiring reliability.
- Cause of degradation: It was shown that the cause of mechanical degradation is morphological changes in the powder. SEM analysis confirmed grain agglomeration resulting from thermal ageing, which worsens material flowability and leads to increased porosity of finished parts.
- Loss of dimensional stability: A significant increase in part shrinkage is observed, leading to a loss of dimensional accuracy. The actual cross-sectional area of samples decreased by 10.57 % after 10 cycles.

Based on the analysis of degradation phases, practical recommendations for the industry were formulated. For the tested hardware and material configuration (Sintratec Kit, PA12), a "safe recycling window" was identified. The powder can be reused 100 % up to 4 cycles, retaining approx. 90 % of the original tensile strength and acceptable process repeatability. Using powder beyond five cycles is associated with a rapid and unpredictable drop in key parameters and is not recommended for functional parts. Despite the decrease in tensile strength, recycled material may find application in the production of elements with damping characteristics, such as prototype vibration isolators, where geometry is key, not just maximum material strength (Knitter et al., 2022; Pecolt et al., 2021).

A direction for further research should be conducting analogous tests for different powder refreshing strategies (e.g. 50 % new material / 50 % used material) to find the optimal compromise between material savings and the quality and reliability of finished parts, also for damping systems (Jereczek et al., 2022; Królikowski et al., 2020; Maciejewski et al., 2022). A prospective direction for further research is the development of a predictive model based on artificial intelligence, analogous to solutions used in modelling the topography of abrasive tools (Bałasz et al., 2007; Stępień et al., 2026), which would allow for automatic classification of the suitability of recycled powder.

Bibliography

Agarwal, H., Singhal, A., & Raj, K. (2021). 3D Printed Quadcopter. In: Saran, V. H., Misra, R. K. (eds.) *Advances in Systems Engineering. Lecture Notes in Mechanical Engineering.* Singapore: Springer.

Alejandro Garcia Rodríguez, Edgar Espejo Mora, Marco Antonio Velasco & Carlos Alberto Narváez Tovar (2023). "Mechanical Properties of Polyamide 12 Manufactured by Means of SLS: Influence of Wall Thickness and Build Direction". Published by IOP Publishing Ltd, *Materials Research Express, 10*(10).

Andries, V. & Zaharia, S.-M., (2025). "Generative Design, Simulation, and 3D Printing of the Quadcopter Drone Frame". *Applied Sciences 15*, 9647.

Attaran, M. (2017). *The Rise of 3-D Printing: The Advantages of Additive Manufacturing Over Traditional Manufacturing.* Business Horizons

Bałasz, B., Szatkiewicz, T., & Królikowski, T. (2007). *Grinding Wheel Topography Modeling with Application of an Elastic Neural Network*, Lecture Notes in Computer Science, 4682, pp. 83–90

Chao Cai, Wei Shian Tey, Jiayao Chen, Wei Zhu, Xingjian Liu, Tong Liu, Lihua Zhao, & Kun Zhou (2021). "Comparative Study on 3D Printing of Polyamide 12 by Selective Laser Sintering and Multi Jet Fusion". *Journal of Materials Processing Technology*, 288, 116882, ISSN 0924-0136.

Dadbakhsh, S., Verbelen, L., Verkinderen, O., Strobbe, D., Van Puyvelde, P., & Kruth, J. P. (2017). "Effect of PA12 Powder Reuse on Coalescence Behaviour and Microstructure of SLS Parts". *European Polymer Journal.*

Dyczkowska, J., Chamier-Gliszczyński, N., Olkiewicz, M., & Królikowski, T. (2023). "Decision Support in the Area of Logistics 4.0". *Procedia Computer Science*, 225, 4758–4765

Dyczkowska J. A., Olkiewicz M., & Królikowski T. (2025) "The Use of Artificial Intelligence in Logistics Information Systems". *Procedia Computer Science*, 270, pp. 5198–5206.

Dyczkowska J., Olkiewicz M., Chamier-Gliszczyński N., & Królikowski T. (2023). "The Range IT Technologies Used in the West Pomeranian Microenterprises". *Procedia Computer Science*, 225, pp. 4110–4118.

Glowinski, S., Pecolt, S., Błażejewski, A., Maciejewski, I., & Królikowski, T. (2025). "Gait Analysis with an Upper Limb Prosthesis in a Child with Thrombocytopenia-Absent Radius Syndrome". *J. Clin. Med.*, 14, 2245.

Gomes, P.C., Piñeiro, O.G., Alves, A.C., & Carneiro, O.S., (2022) "On the Reuse of SLS Polyamide 12 Powder". *Materials*, 15, 5486.

Grunt M., Błażejewski A., Pecolt S., & Królikowski T. (2022). "BelBuk System Smart Logistics for Sustainable City Development in Terms of the Deficit of a Chemical Fertilizers". *Energies*, *15*(13).

Jana Machotová, Marek Pagáč, Roman Svoboda, Jan Jansa, Štěpán Podzimek, Eva Černošková, Jiří Palarčík, Zuzana Koutová, Petr Kutálek, & Lucie Zárybnická (2024). "Effect of PA12 Powder Recycling on Properties of SLS 3D Printed Parts Including Their Hygroscopicity". *European Polymer Journal*, 220, 113432, ISSN 14–3057.

Jereczek, B., Maciejewski, I., Krzyzynski, T., & Królikowski, T., (2022). "Modeling and Simulation of the Horizontal Seat Suspension System Under Random Vibration". *Procedia Computer Science*, 207, 858–866

Kantaros, A., Drosos, C., Papoutsidakis, M., Pallis, E., & Ganetsos, T. (2025). "Composite Filament Materials for 3D-Printed Drone Parts: Advancements in Mechanical Strength, Weight Optimization and Embedded Electronics". *Materials*, 18, 2465

Kateb, F., Haseeb, A., Misbah-Un-Noor, S., Alghamdi, B.M., Khan, F.Q., Khan, B., Baseer, A., Marwat, M.I., & Jan, S. (2025). "Drone Frame Optimization via Simulation and 3D Printing". *Computers*, *14*, 328.

Kohutiar, M., Kakošová, L., Krbata, M., Janík, R., Fekiaˇc, J.J., Breznická, A., Eckert, M., Mikuš, P., & Timárová, L. (2025). "Comprehensive Review: Technological Approaches, Properties, and Applications of Pure and Reinforced Polyamide 6 (PA6) and Polyamide 12 (PA12)". *Composite Materials. Polymers*, *17*, 442.

Koren, Y. (2010). *The Global Manufacturing Revolution: Product-Process-Business Integration and Reconfigurable Systems*. John Wiley & Sons.

Kostrzewski, M., Sompolski, K., & Królikowski, T., (2022). "How Profitable Is It to Apply Industry 4.0 Solutions in Blister Factories?". *Procedia Computer Science*, 207, pp. 3275–3283

Królikowski, T., Błażejewski, A., & Knitter, R. (2020). "Optimization of Multilayer Rail Substrate under Moving Load, Using Metamaterials". *Procedia Computer Science*, 176, pp. 3399–3406

Knitter R., Błażejewski A., & Królikowski T. (2022). "Modeling and Simulation of Vibro-isolator Rapid Prototyping Using Additive Manufacturing". *Procedia Computer Science*, 207, pp. 1293–1302.

Królikowski T., Bałasz B., & Ubowska A., (2021). "Dynamics of Changes in Poland in the Light of the Industry 4.0," *Procedia Computer Science*, 192, pp. 4128–4137.

Królikowski T., Strulak-Wójcikiewicz R., Nikończuk P., Zmuda Trzebiatowski P., & Deja A., (2020). "Small-lot Production with Additive Production Using Reverse Logistics and IT Solutions in COVID-19 Era". *European Research Studies Journal*, XXIII(2), pp. 569–579.

Królikowski T., Knitter R., Błażejewski A., Glowinski S., & Kamiński K., (2019). "Emission of Particles and VOCs at 3D Printing in Automotive". *Sustainable Design and Manufacturing (SDM19)*, Springer, pp. 485–495.

Królikowski T., Knitter R., & Stachnik M., (2019). "Thermo-mechanic Tests Using 3d Printed Elements," *Procedia Computer Science*, 159, pp. 2551–2559

Królikowski T., Knitter R., & Błażejewski A. (2019). "Computer Modeling and Testing of Structural Metamaterials". *Procedia Computer Science*, 159, pp. 2543–2550

Królikowski T., & Mikulski K. (2024). "Laboratoria przyszłości w edukacji w kontekście proksemiki," *Wydawnictwo Uczelniane WSG: Bydgoszcz*.

Kruth, J.P., Leu, M.C., & Nakagawa, T. (1998). “Progress in Additive Manufacturing and Rapid Prototyping”. *CIRP Annals – Manufacturing Technology*, *47*, 525–540.

Kumar, S. (2003). “Selective Laser Sintering: A Qualitative and Objective Approach”. *JOM (formerly Journal of The Minerals, Metals & Materials Society)* 55, 43–47.

Khoshsepehr, Z., Alinejad, S., Solookian-Jahromi, F., & Ebrahimi, S. (2026). A novel decomposed fuzzy approach for addressing Industry 5.0 challenges in smart-sustainable circular supply chain management. Advanced Engineering Informatics, 69(Part C), Article 104036. https://doi.org/10.1016/j.aei.2025.104036

Khoshsepehr, Z., Alinejad, S., Solookian-Jahromi, F., & Ebrahimi, S. (2026). A novel decomposed fuzzy approach for addressing Industry 5.0 challenges in smart-sustainable circular supply chain management. Advanced Engineering Informatics, 69, Article 104036. https://doi.org/10.1016/j.aei.2025.104036

Machała S., Chamier-Gliszczyński N., & Królikowski T., (2022). “Application of AR/VR Technology in Industry 4.0,” *Procedia Computer Science*, 207, pp. 2984–2992.

Muhamad Damanhuri, A. A., Hariri, A., Alkahari, M. R., Md Fauadi, M. H. F., & Zainal Bakri, S. F. (2019). Indoor air concentration from selective laser sintering 3D printer using virgin polyamide nylon (PA12) powder: A pilot study. International Journal of Integrated Engineering, 11(5), 140–149. https://doi.org/10.30880/ijie.2019.11.05.019

Machała S., Królikowski T., & Chamier-Gliszczyński N. (2023). “Application of Smart Watches for Monitoring the Health State of Professional Drivers”. *Procedia Computer Science*, 225, pp. 4084–4091.

Maciejewski, I., Błażejewski, A., Pecolt, S., & Królikowski, T. (2022). “Multibody Model Simulating Biodynamic Response of the Seated Human under Whole-Body Vibration”. *Procedia Computer Science*, 207, 227–234.

Malik˙ enait˙ e, G., Rimkus, A., Rudinskas, D., Jukna, A., & Gribniak, V., (2025). “Additive Manufacturing of Conductive Pathways for Drone Electrical Equipment”. *Polymers*, 17, 1452.

Mielicki, C., Gronhoff, B., & Wortberg, J. (2014). “Effects of Laser Sintering Processing Time and Temperature on Changes in Polyamide 12 Powder Particle Size, Shape and Distribution”. *AIP Conference Proceedings* 1593 (1): 728–731. <https://doi.org/10.1063/1.4873880>

MohamedZain, A.O., Chua, H., Yap, K., Uthayasurian, P., & Jiehan, T. (2022). "Novel Drone Design Using an Optimization Software with 3D Model, Simulation, and Fabrication in Drone Systems Research". *Drones*, 6, 97.

Omar, M.R. et al. (2022). Effects of Different Polyamide (PAa12) Composition on Dimensional Accuracy in Selective Laser Sintering. In: Abdollah, M.F.B., Amiruddin, H., Phuman Singh, A.S., Abdul Munir, F., Ibrahim, A. (eds) *Proceedings of the 7th International Conference and Exhibition on Sustainable Energy and Advanced Materials (ICE-SEAM 2021), Melaka, Malaysia. ICE-SEAM 2021. Lecture Notes in Mechanical Engineering. Springer, Singapore*. https://doi.org/10.1007/978-981-19-3179-6_7

Pecolt, S., Błażejewski, A., Królikowski, T., Trzebiatowski, P.Z., & Schulz, B. (2021). "Autonomous Control of a Mobile Robot to Explore Areas with Difficult Terrain". *Procedia Computer Science Open Source Preview*, 192, 3467–3476

Prakhyat Hejmady, Lambèrt C.A. van Breemen, Daniel Hermida-Merino, Patrick D. Anderson, & Ruth Cardinaels, (2022). "Laser Sintering of PA12 Particles Studied by In-Situ Optical, Thermal and X-ray Characterization," *Additive Manufacturing*, 52, 102624.

Šostakaitė, L., Šapranauskas, E., Rudinskas, D., Rimkus, A., & Gribniak, V. (2024). "Investigating Additive Manufacturing Possibilities for an Unmanned Aerial Vehicle with Polymeric Materials". *Polymers* 16, 2600.

Stępień, P., Bałasz, B., Szatkiewicz, T., & Królikowski, T. (2006). "Application of Artificial Intelligence Algorithms for the Modeling of the Surfaces of Abrasive Grains". In *4th International Industrial Simulation Conference 2006 Isc*, pp. 265–268

Tomasz, K., Remigiusz, K., Andrzej, B., Jerzy, Z., & Aleksander, B. (2021). "Industry 4.0– Supporting Industry in Design Solutions– All-in-one Computer Cover". *Smart Innovation Systems and Technologies*, 200, 93–105

Wudy, K., Drummer, D., Kühnlein, F., & Drexler, M. (2014). "Influence of Degradation Behavior of Polyamide 12 Powders in Laser Sintering Process on Produced Parts". *AIP Conference Proceedings* 1593 (1): 691–695. <https://doi.org/10.1063/1.4873873>

Zmuda Trzebiatowski, P., Królikowski, T., Ubowska, A., & Wasilewski, K. (2025). Reverse Engineering as a Tool of Protection of Cultural Heritage. A Case Study. *Proceedings of the International Conference on Knowledge-Based and Intelligent Information & Engineering Systems (KES)*.

Zmuda Trzebiatowski, P., Królikowski, T., Ubowska, A., & Wilpiszewska, K. (2025). "Preparation and Properties of PETG Filament Modified with a Metallic Additive". *Materials*, 18, 1203.

AI and gender, racial, and ethnic inequalities in workspaces

Dominika Liszkowska[1]

ABSTRACT

As artificial intelligence (AI) technology continues to evolve, its impact on the labour market remains multifaceted and complex. Recent advances in this field have raised concerns, including that the technology could automate many human tasks, leading to a significant decline in labour demand, lower wages, and limited employment opportunities. Another significant concern is the neutrality of AI. Numerous studies confirm that this technology not only perpetuates prejudices, leading to discrimination and marginalisation of certain categories of workers. It also has disproportionate and negative effects on social groups that have historically faced the greatest obstacles in the labour market. The purpose of this chapter is to demonstrate how AI is impacting the labour market, which is linked to historical patterns of social inequality related to gender, race, and ethnicity.

Keywords: Artificial intelligence, labour market, gender, race, ethnicity

Introduction

In recent years, technological transformation, a permanent feature of modern socio-economic systems, has gained enormous momentum. This is primarily due to the dynamic development of artificial intelligence (AI), especially generative artificial intelligence (GenAI) (Troszyński et al., 2025, p. 5), which is now one of the key elements of the digital revolution. Artificial intelligence is defined as "the ability of something like a machine to understand, learn, and interpret on its own in a human-like manner" (Chen, 2023, p. 4). It is a collective term that encompasses a wide range of models, methods, and frameworks used to simulate human intelligence, often in the context of collecting, processing, and using data (Köchling & Wehner, 2020, p. 798). The term "transformation," in turn, means transforming something or transforming it into something else and refers to various areas of knowledge and practice in socio-economic life. Transformation is therefore understood as striving for something different, new, and at the same time distinct from what has existed so far. Compared to the current state, however, the scale of this change will

1 Faculty of Humanities, Koszalin University of Technology, ORCID: 0000-0001-6312-341X.

be significant and, in civilisational terms, may lead to the achievement of a new, higher stage of development (Bielińska-Dusza, 2022, p. 191).

As a result of the increasing dynamics of AI tools, negative attitudes toward this technology are emerging, and concerns are growing about its impact on the labour market, among other things. AI's potential translates into the ability to create new applications and innovations in various sectors, which could contribute to profound and long-term socio-economic changes (Troszyński et al., 2025, p. 5). AI therefore plays a significant role in analysing current labour market trends, forecasting future competency needs (future competencies), and talent management. Some researchers and analysts link the increased use of AI and robots with a decline in employment and wages. They believe the rapid pace of change will lead to the automation of numerous professions worldwide, resulting in the disappearance of far more jobs than are created. According to these projections, AI is expected to displace approximately one-third of existing jobs globally within a decade, with the economies of the United States (US) and Japan being particularly hard hit (Klimek, 2025, p. 5).

On the other hand, emerging analyses show that AI, rather than simply replacing jobs, will create new opportunities and transform existing roles. According to forecasts from the World Economic Forum, artificial intelligence and automation will create 69 million new jobs worldwide by 2028. In this context, the importance of upskilling and reskilling programmes is emphasised, as future roles and tasks will require employees to acquire new skills in areas such as data analysis, machine learning, artificial intelligence development, and creative thinking (International Economic Development Council, 2025, p. 5).

The purpose of this chapter is to demonstrate the impact of AI on the labour market in the context of perpetuating and deepening social inequalities related to gender, race, and ethnicity. Implementing AI systems in recruitment, selection, job evaluation, and promotion processes is often justified by the desire to increase efficiency and objectify decisions. However, AI technologies operate based on historical data and design assumptions that reflect existing power structures and patterns of exclusion present in the labour market. Consequently, AI algorithms can not only reproduce previous forms of discrimination but also reinforce them and transform them into individual prejudices.

This analysis aims to answer three main research questions: (1) How do AI systems shape the functioning of contemporary labour markets? (2) To what extent does AI contribute to the reproduction or amplification of existing social inequalities and discriminatory patterns in the labour market? (3) How do algorithmic decision-making systems affect access to employment and career development opportunities? To answer these questions, a descriptive and explanatory analysis was conducted. Its goal is to both describe the phenomenon of AI use in the labour market and to explain the mechanisms leading to the deepening of inequalities and discrimination.

AI and the challenges of discrimination and inequality

Artificial intelligence is being implemented at an accelerating pace in key areas of modern society, from healthcare and justice, through public services, to recruitment processes and human resources management (Fernández-Prados et al., 2025, p. 59). This phenomenon should be analysed in the broader context of discrimination, which, however, is not a general concept. It concerns socially significant categories that have historically provided the basis for unjustified and systematically unfavourable treatment based on possession of a protected characteristic, commonly recognised as race, gender, religion, disability, or place of birth (Barocas et al., 2019, p. 52).

The literature distinguishes two main dimensions of discrimination: direct and indirect. The former refers to situations in which an individual is treated less favourably than another individual or group of individuals because they possess a protected characteristic. It also encompasses cases in which an individual is discriminated against because they are attributed such a characteristic (discrimination by perception) or because of their association with a person possessing a protected characteristic (discrimination by association) (Equality and Human Rights Commission, 2019). Direct discrimination occurs when an individual is treated less favourably than another person in a comparable situation because of one of the protected characteristics. This is easily identifiable because it is based on explicit and intentional discriminatory acts. In the case of direct discrimination, victims have clear grounds to pursue their rights in court or before the bodies responsible for their protection (Asistwork, 2025).

The situation of people experiencing indirect discrimination is somewhat more difficult to identify and prove. This type of treatment occurs when seemingly neutral regulations or practices lead to unfavourable treatment of a given individual or a specific group of people. Proving the existence of indirect discrimination requires demonstrating a causal relationship and a detailed analysis of the regulations or policies in place with negative consequences for a given individual or group (Asistwork, 2025). In other words,

> indirect discrimination aims to capture cases where a rule, policy, or measure is apparently neutral, does not necessarily rely on any bias or intention to discriminate, and yet produces a significant disadvantage for members of a protected group when compared with a cognate group (Cossette-Lefebvre & Maclure, 2023, p. 1257).

An example of direct discrimination would be refusing to hire an individual based on race, national or ethnic origin, physical or mental disability, skin colour, religion, gender, or age. Indirect discrimination (disparate impact discrimination) could refer to a situation where a high school diploma is required for a position where it is not required for proper performance of job duties. Such a seemingly neutral requirement may, in practice, disproportionately exclude a specific individual or group if there is no objective justification for its application (Cossette-Lefebvre & Maclure, 2023, p. 1256).

One of the main problems related to the operation of AI in many social and economic aspects is the issue of so-called algorithmic discrimination (Kulesza, 2023). As Hugo Cossette-Lefebvre and Jocelyn Maclure note, the use of algorithms can be a source of erroneous discriminatory decisions due to at least one of three characteristics attributed to algorithms: (1) the data mining process and the categorisation on which they are based can reconstruct human prejudices; (2) the automaticity of algorithms and their predictive design can lead to relying on erroneous generalisations; (3) the opaque nature of algorithms contradicts the requirements of democracy (Cossette-Lefebvre & Maclure, 2023, p. 1255).

Artificial intelligence systems' use of historical data, loaded with subjective biases, allows algorithms to learn patterns of discrimination present in training data, internalise them, and then reproduce them in automated decision-making processes (Hall & Clapton, 2021, p. 8). The impartiality of conclusions drawn by AI applications therefore depends, firstly, on the quality and completeness of the datasets used, and secondly, on the assumptions built into the algorithms responsible for searching, selecting, and analysing information. As a result of data errors, the datasets used may be incomplete and distorted, failing to convey a complete picture of the phenomenon being analysed. This leads to favouring certain social groups while ignoring or marginalising the representation of others. Furthermore, prior interpretations of data may contain hidden cognitive biases that reinforce false conclusions, including prejudices and stereotypes related to gender, race, ethnicity, or other social characteristics. Such errors can be directly encoded in the design of the decision-making algorithms themselves, thus contributing to the perpetuation of existing forms of discrimination (Matlin et al., 2025, p. 4). Artificial intelligence is therefore not only a technological force, but also a deeply sociotechnical tool that reflects existing social structures, norms and inequalities, and at the same time actively co-creates them and profoundly influences them (Maafo, 2025, pp. 1306–1307).

Another significant problem underlying bias and discriminatory practices in AI relates to the demographic profile and lack of diversity among the programmers, engineers, and technicians who create this technology. As Lucy Hall and William Clapton note, historically, the lack of representation among those with the means to create advanced technologies has often had serious and negative consequences for groups not involved in the process (Hall & Clapton, 2021, p. 8). The lack of racial and gender diversity and the concentration of power in a few locations in AI production and research thus contribute to the systematic discrimination of already marginalised populations. The lack of diverse perspectives in AI development raises serious concerns about bias, lack of representation, and social justice (Pal et al., 2024).

This problem was described by Joy Buolamwini in her concept of "exclusion overhead." It highlights the additional burdens and costs that individuals must bear when technological systems are not designed with their needs or characteristics in mind. For example, an AI-based facial recognition system developed by men may have limited recognition of women's faces, especially those of diverse ethnic backgrounds. Furthermore, the additional burdens resulting from the exclusion of women and minorities can increase the risk of identification errors and system failures, leading to practical problems in areas such as security checks and access to devices and services (Pal et al., 2024). This includes in the workplace.

This conclusion is also supported by the Gender Shades project, conducted in 2018. Using an intersectional approach, three commercial gender classification algorithms were evaluated, including those developed by IBM and Microsoft. For the analysis, the subjects were divided into four groups: (1) darker-skinned women, (2) darker-skinned men, (3) lighter-skinned women, and (4) lighter-skinned men. For all three algorithms, darker-skinned women performed worse, with error rates up to 34 % higher than lighter-skinned men. These conclusions were subsequently confirmed by an independent evaluation by experts at the National Institute of Standards and Technology (NIST). The evaluation found that the facial recognition systems in the 189 algorithms tested were the least accurate at identifying darker-skinned women (Najibi, 2020). Another example is systems used for automatic facial recognition by law enforcement. A study conducted across 100 police departments in the United States found that agencies using facial recognition systems are more likely to stop and search African Americans than members of other ethnic groups (Buolamwini & Gebru, 2018, p. 2).

The demographic profile of AI developers, which is often homogenous in terms of gender, race, and ethnicity, can reflect and reinforce existing social biases, not just in the technology industry. These consequences extend far beyond the technology industry and permeate social interactions facilitated by AI systems in institutions and services. An example is a study by Yanbo Ge et al., which analysed the behaviour of UberX and Lyft drivers toward Black passengers (Barocas et al., 2019, pp. 205–207). In Seattle, African American passengers had to wait up to 35 % longer for transportation than other passengers. In Boston, discrimination by Uber drivers manifested itself in nearly twice as many cancellations for passengers with African American-sounding names as for those from other groups. Additionally, men using African American names in the app when requesting a ride in sparsely populated areas were more than three times more likely to have their ride cancelled (Ge et al., 2016).

As Rifat Ara Shams, Didar Zowghi, and Muneera Bano note, integrating the principles of diversity and inclusion has the potential to mitigate the challenges stemming from the lack of fairness and bias associated with AI. As numerous studies demonstrate, from a technology design perspective, diverse teams have the potential to bring diverse perspectives and can identify additional sources of bias embedded in algorithms. Including marginalised groups in the design and development of AI systems increases the likelihood of creating more equitable algorithms and strengthens trust in the technology. Therefore, the design, development, and implementation of AI systems should be guided by the principles of diversity and inclusion. Therefore, when done correctly, AI can serve as a tool to support the improvement and acceleration of practices, as well as the understanding of diversity and inclusion in various spheres of life (Shams et al., 2025).

Artificial Intelligence and the labour market

In the context of the dynamic changes associated with the development of artificial intelligence, three key areas of uncertainty can be identified. First, it is unclear how AI technologies could replace or complement work previously performed by humans in specific tasks and professions. Consequently, this situation may ultimately contribute to the structural segmentation of the labour market and foster the emergence of groups of beneficiaries and groups particularly vulnerable to the negative effects of automation. Second, there is the issue of varying exposure to AI across states, particularly the systematic differences between developed economies and emerging markets. Third, within individual economies, exposure to the risks and benefits of AI also vary depending on demographic groups and skill levels. This significantly complicates forecasting the implications for economic disparities, which may intensify with the widespread adoption of AI-based solutions (Pizzinelli et al., 2023, p. 1). For example, a 2022 study by Nobel laureate Daron Acemoğlu and his colleagues found that while AI adoption initially increased employment in related industries, it soon led to fewer jobs and a shift in skill requirements in many companies. This finding suggests that in vulnerable sectors, the "substitution effect" may begin to outweigh the "income effect." In another study, the same group of researchers found that income inequality has increased as a result of automation, further revealing how unequal the job market, based on skills and the impact of AI, may be in the coming years (Pozzi et al., 2025).

Historical experience shows that changes in the labour market accompanying successive waves of technological progress – from agricultural mechanisation, through industrial automation, to the digital revolution (Gracea & Okoh, 2022, p. 24) – have each brought with them a so-called "extension effect." According to this concept, technology increases employee productivity and, at the same time, creates new roles, often offsetting job losses through increased demand and income. However, as numerous observations suggest, this is neither a painless nor immediate process and may undergo numerous changes in the era of AI implementation. The constant evolution of technological innovations, and the emergence of artificial intelligence in particular, have profoundly transformed the structure and dynamics of the labour market. This is reflected in the changing nature of work, professional roles, and employment dynamics across various industries. The implications of AI development for the labour market are therefore complex and multifaceted. On the one hand, AI has the potential to automate tasks, improve decision-making processes, and create new employment opportunities in areas such as machine learning and data analysis (International Economic Development Council, 2025, p. 3). On the other hand, it raises concerns about ethics, worker migration, and skill polarisation. Furthermore, AI's uniqueness lies in its ability not only to automate physical tasks but also to replicate numerous cognitive functions, including pattern recognition and decision-making, which until recently were considered the exclusive domain of humans. This shift is therefore ushering in a new phase of disruption in the labour market, where the boundaries between human and machine capabilities are becoming increasingly blurred (Gracea & Okoh, 2022, p. 24).

The transformations that AI is bringing to the labour market are raising both hopes and concerns. One of the most obvious benefits for the labour market seems to be increased productivity. Implementing this technology significantly shortens the execution time of processes that were previously time-consuming and required long hours of engagement. AI can also quickly analyse data and adapt to it in real time, which in turn translates into a significant improvement in the quality of services provided. Automation of many processes also reduces costs, including the human resources required to perform routine tasks. Therefore, companies that decide to implement AI-based solutions can become more competitive in the market, and employees can focus on tasks requiring a higher level of commitment, creativity, and competence (EY Academy of Business, 2025). At the same time, however, research indicates that approximately 40 % of employers worldwide already declare their intention to reduce headcount in areas where AI can take over some responsibilities previously performed by employees. This scale may illustrate the scope of planned organisational changes and the potential impact of AI on the employment structure (Kubera, 2025).

Artificial intelligence, discrimination, and the deepening of labour market inequalities

A crucial dimension of contemporary technological transformation is the intersection of categories such as artificial intelligence and gender, which is particularly evident in the labour market. This relationship is ambivalent. On the one hand, AI has significant potential to be a powerful catalyst for promoting gender equality and women's empowerment, offering numerous tools aimed at closing gaps in healthcare, education, and economic opportunities. On the other hand, if AI is implemented and developed without careful consideration of gender dynamics, the potential to perpetuate and reinforce, or even create new forms of prejudice and discrimination could deepen existing inequalities (Maafo, 2025, pp. 1306–1307).

Analysing the relationship between AI and gender allows us to identify the mechanisms through which algorithmic technologies influence unequal access for women and men to employment, career advancement, and job security. The first problem is the significant underrepresentation of women and other marginalised groups throughout the AI development process and industry. This occurs from the educational pathways, through research labs and corporate development teams, to management positions (Maafo, 2025, pp. 1306–1307). Research by Judy Wajcman's team shows that only 22 % of data and AI professionals in the UK are women, with this percentage dropping to 8 % for specialists and researchers attending major machine-learning conferences (The Alan Turing Institute, 2021). Research by Siddhi Pal, Ruggero Marino Lazzaroni, and Paul Mendoza also shows that of the nearly 1.6 million AI professionals worldwide, only 22 % are women. Their representation in management positions is also lower, at just 14 %. Published data reveals significant disparities in the AI sector in the European Union as well. While states like Latvia and Finland have female representation in AI exceeding 40 % (45.3 % and 43.3 %, respectively), large economies like Germany lag significantly behind. And while Germany, along with France and the Netherlands, has one of the highest absolute numbers of women with AI skills, women only make up 20.3 % of AI specialists there. Among

EU member states, this figure is surpassed only by Austria, where the share of women among AI specialists is just 19.4 % (Pal et al., 2024).

Numerous studies indicate that insufficient diversity among AI system developers is closely linked to the problem of perpetuating biases in the labour market, which become embedded in algorithms and can lead to systematic discrimination against specific groups. AI tools, which are often characterised by a lack of neutrality, often reflect the perspectives and values of their creators (Pal et al., 2024). This creates a kind of feedback loop, where social biases are implemented in machine-learning systems and then perpetuated and intensified systemically. This process is a consequence of poor quality or biased training data, model design errors, and deficiencies in their evaluation, leading to the generation of discriminatory results (Maafo, 2025, pp. 1306–1307).

These mechanisms were also confirmed by the results of analyses conducted by Lina Dencik, which showed that the use of AI in the workplace discriminates against employees from ethnic minorities, Black people, and Asians. This discrimination occurs in both direct and indirect ways. As the author of the report on AI Inequalities at Workprojekt notes, some artificial intelligence models do not explicitly consider demographic data related to ethnicity. Others, however, can act as precise indicators of such characteristics, leading to direct forms of discrimination. Data categories such as names and surnames, language of communication, and postal codes function in practice as indicators of ethnicity, so their use in decision-making systems results in discrimination against employees belonging to ethnic minorities (Williams & Dencik, 2025).

This form of discrimination can occur as early as the recruitment process. Zhisheng Chen's research, for example, has shown that AI-assisted recruitment has the potential to improve recruitment quality, enhance operational efficiency, and reduce the burden of transactional work. However, due to algorithmic bias, discriminatory practices often occur. These biases apply to categories such as gender, race, and skin colour, stemming from both limited data sets and the bias of technology developers (Chen, 2023, p. 1). Data-related errors arise when AI models use them, as historical data largely reflects previous recruitment trends, favouring certain demographic groups. Consequently, AI systems can perpetuate these patterns and replicate practices that lead to discrimination (Chhatre & Singh, 2025, p. 466).

Another example in the early stages of recruitment is HR chatbots, which utilise a specific database of employee language phrases to conduct conversations. These systems often struggle to understand written or spoken language that deviates from the dominant group's (e.g. white employees). Analyses have shown that speech recognition tools across all major technology vendors had significantly higher error rates for Black individuals, indicating the risk of perpetuating existing biases in recruitment processes (Williams & Dencik, 2025). Similarly, research by Eve Fleisig et al. on ChatGPT's use of English revealed that language models default to "standard" English. Conversely, when non-standard language variants were used, the chatbot exhibited greater stereotyping (19 %), used more demeaning and offensive content (25 %), had poorer context understanding (9 %), and used a condescending tone (15 %). Moreover, when the models were asked to imitate a non-standard style, the text they generated was characterised by a lower degree of input data understanding and a greater susceptibility to stereotyping (Fleisig et al., 2024, p. 13541).

This isn't the only mechanism by which AI systems can perpetuate existing inequalities. Women and other marginalised groups attempting to pursue careers in AI face a number of additional structural and cultural barriers. These include a hostile organisational culture, significant gaps in access to financing, persistent wage inequalities, and limited access to mentoring and sponsorship (Maafo, 2025, pp. 1306–1307). Satyam Mohla, Bishnupriya Bagh, and Anupam Guha point out in their analyses that employment inequalities related to AI stem largely from material conditions, including the concentration of capital that determines technology development (Mohla et al., 2024, p. 2). To illustrate this problem, the authors cite historical data showing that in the 1970s, women constituted a significant portion of computer science students and played a significant role in the development of the field. A prominent example is the Brazilian Institute of Mathematics and Statistics (IME) at the University of São Paulo (USP), where in 1974, fourteen of the twenty students who graduated from the first computer science program were women. In the 1980s, the percentage of women with computer science degrees began to drop below 40 %. According to data from the National Center for Education Statistics in the US, between 1984 and 1985, women constituted almost 37 % of all undergraduate computer science students (Rodrigo de Oliveira Andrade, 2019).

According to researchers analysing the connections between science, technology and gender, this change was a result of the perception of computer science studies themselves. Initially, computer science (including programming) was associated with office work that did not require high qualifications. In the following years (especially at the beginning of the twenty-first century), the cultural, social, and economic growth of this field revealed a trend in which women were less and less often identified with IT positions (Mohla et al., 2024, p. 2). Ana Matsusaki, in turn, points to the emergence and rapid dissemination of personal computers in the mid-1980s as a significant factor in this change. Data shows that boys in the US, being the main marketing target of manufacturers, used computers at home much more frequently than girls, which may have led to their greater interest in the subject and programming. Thus, "the notion that programming was a masculine activity became the standard narrative, and the names of many women who made important contributions to the field were forgotten" (Rodrigo de Oliveira Andrade, 2019).

Today, these conditions not only hinder women's professional development in the IT industry but also contribute to increased turnover. In turn, the implementation of AI-based technologies impacts women's lives differently compared to men. This applies to employment prospects, economic security, required qualifications and skills (Maafo, 2025, pp. 1306–1307), as well as daily work experiences, including interactions with algorithmic employee evaluation, monitoring, and selection systems.

Conclusion

In the context of the growing importance of AI in the labour market, forms of discrimination and inequality in employment are taking on a new dimension. Considering the typology of forms of discrimination in the labour market, firstly, AI and algorithms can reinforce employment discrimination (Pacian et al., 2012, pp. 79–80). This occurs when, despite comparable qualifications and professional competences, certain individuals or social groups are affected by unequal participation in employment or unemployment. Such inequalities often emerge already at the recruitment stage. In such cases, algorithms produce discriminatory or biased results due to unrepresentative input data. An example of such a mechanism was the case of Amazon, which used AI systems in its recruitment processes. The algorithms used by the corporation systematically generated unfavourable results for female candidates. Consequently, the use of AI tools to support hiring decisions was abandoned (Köchling & Wehner, 2020, pp. 796–797).

Secondly, algorithmically restricting access to certain professions through the use of arbitrary or overly restrictive selection criteria, which are not always truly necessary for the job, leads to the strengthening of qualification-based and occupational discrimination. This includes criteria such as required educational paths, specific types of professional experience, and the requirement for continuous employment history (Pacian et al., 2012, pp. 79–80). Using AI in the recruitment process, a highly qualified candidate whose CV is missing several keywords can be automatically rejected before their application reaches human review (Tracey et al., 2025). Furthermore, the data used to train the algorithm, reflecting biased recruitment patterns and perpetuating prejudice, can favour individuals of a certain gender, race, age group, or alumni of a given institution. This can filter out qualified candidates simply because they don't fit the profile the algorithm has learned to prefer, such as women applying for technical or management positions.

Marginalised groups also experience "human capital" discrimination, which occurs when some individuals have limited access to productivity-enhancing factors such as education, vocational training, or practical experience. An example of the indirect impact of AI on this type of discrimination is when AI systems predicting various aspects of a candidate's job use their postal code to determine the distance between their home and the workplace. Due to historical patterns of residential segregation, postcodes can act as a proxy for race or social status (although these categories are not included in the model at all). Individuals belonging to historically excluded groups residing in certain neighbourhoods may be systematically underestimated in terms of their projected potential, limiting their access to training, promotions, and other career opportunities (Capasso et al., 2024, p. 349).

The use of AI in recruitment and human resources management therefore poses a structural risk of exacerbating existing inequalities in the labour market. Historically, marginalised groups are particularly vulnerable. As the analysis shows, although algorithms are often perceived as neutral and objective tools, their operation is deeply embedded in the social, institutional, and data contexts that shape them. Therefore, it is crucial that combating algorithmic discrimination utilises not only technical solutions but also appropriate regulatory frameworks, transparent decision-making processes, and critical reflection on the role of AI in shaping the future of the labour market.

Bibliography

Asistwork (2025). *Dyskryminacja posrednia i bezposrednia – poznaj roznice i przyklady* [Direct and indirect discrimination – learn the differences and examples]. Accessed December 31, 2025. <https://praca.asistwork.pl/blog/prawo-pracy/dyskryminacja-posrednia-i-bezposrednia-poznaj-roznice-i-przyklady>.

Barocas, S., et al. (2019). *Fairness and Machine Learning: Limitations and Opportunities*. Accessed December 31, 2025. <https://fairmlbook.org/pdf/fairmlbook.pdf>.

Bielinska-Dusza, E. (2022). "Transformacja technologiczna przedsiebiorstw jako skutek zastosowania sztucznej inteligencji" [Technological transformation of enterprises as a result of the application of artificial intelligence]. *Organizacja i Kierowanie, 2*(191), 189–208.

Buolamwini, J., & Gebru, T. (2018). "Gender Shades: Intersectional Accuracy Disparities in Commercial Gender Classification". *Proceedings of Machine Learning Research, 81*, 77–91.

Capasso, M., et al. (2024). "On the Right to Work in the Age of Artificial Intelligence: Ethical Safeguards in Algorithmic Human Resource Management." *Business and Human Rights Journal, 9*(3), 346–360.

Chen, Z. (2023). "Ethics and Discrimination in Artificial Intelligence-enabled Recruitment Practices." *Humanities and Social Sciences Communications, 10*(567).

Chhatre, R., & Singh, S. (2025). "Mitigating Bias in AI-Driven Recruitment: Ethical Challenges and Governance Solutions." *Journal of Information Systems Engineering and Management, 10*(48), 462–469.

Cossette-Lefebvre, H., & Maclure, J. (2023). "AI's Fairness Problem: Understanding Wrongful Discrimination in the Context of Automated Decision-making." *AI Ethics, 3*, 1255–1269.

Equality and Human Rights Commission (2019). *Direct and Indirect Discrimination*. Accessed December 31, 2025. <https://www.equalityhumanrights.com/equality/equality-act-2010/your-rights-under-equality-act-2010/direct-and-indirect-discrimination>.

EY Academy of Business (2025). *Wplyw sztucznej inteligencji na przyszlosc pracy* [The Impact of Artificial Intelligence on the Future of Work].

Accessed December 31, 2025. <https://www.academyofbusiness.pl/wplyw-sztucznej-inteligencji-na-przyszlosc-pracy/>.

Fernández-Prados, J. S., et al. (2025). "Racial/Ethnic Bias in AI Systems: A PRISMA Systematic Review of Magnitude, Domains, and Mitigation Strategies (2014–2025)." *International Journal of Migration Studies, 15*(1), 57–81.

Fleisig, E., et al. (2024). "Linguistic Bias in ChatGPT: Language Models Reinforce Dialect Discrimination." *Proceedings of the 2024 Conference on Empirical Methods in Natural Language Processing*, 13541–13564.

Ge, Y., et al. (2016). *Racial and Gender Discrimination in Transportation Network Companies*. NBER Working Paper No. 22776. Accessed December 31, 2025. <https://www.nber.org/system/files/working_papers/w22776/w22776.pdf>.

Gracea, I., & Okoh, O. F. (2022). "The Impact of Artificial Intelligence on Labor Markets and Wage Inequality: A Computational Economic Perspective." *Acta Electronica Malaysia, 6*(1), 24–31.

Hall, L., & Clapton, W. (2021). "Programming the Machine: Gender, Race, Sexuality, AI, and the Construction of Credibility and Deceit at the Border." *Internet Policy Review, 10*(4).

International Economic Development Council (2025). *Artificial Intelligence Impact on Labor Markets: Literature Review*. Washington, DC: IEDC.

Klimek, J. (2025). *Wykorzystanie sztucznej inteligencji na rynku pracy – szanse i wyzwania* [The use of artificial intelligence in the labor market – opportunities and challenges]. Accessed December 31, 2025. <https://izba.wroc.pl/wp-content/uploads/2025/03/Wykorzystanie-sztucznej-inteligencji-na-rynku-pracy.pdf>.

Köchling, A., & Wehner, M. C. (2020). "Discriminated by an Algorithm: A Systematic Review of Discrimination and Fairness by Algorithmic Decision-making in the Context of HR Recruitment and HR Development." *Business Research*, 13, 795–848.

Kubera, G. (2025). *Czy warto jeszcze studiowac? Sztuczna inteligencja a przyszlosc pracy umyslowej* [Is it still worth studying? Artificial Intelligence and the Future of White-Collar Work]. Accessed December 31, 2025. <https://businessinsider.com.pl/technologie/nowe-technologie/automatyzacja-niszczy-rynek-pracy-ai-odbiera-prace-juniorom/nydr85d>.

Kulesza, J. (2023). *Blad w algorytmie – sztuczna inteligencja i dyskryminacja* [Error in the algorithm – artificial intelligence and discrimination]. Accessed December 31, 2025. <https://www.uni.lodz.pl/aktualnosc/szczegoly/blad-w-algorytmie-sztuczna-inteligencja-i-dyskryminacja>.

Maafo, I. K. (2025). "Bridging the Divide: Women, AI, and the Quest for Equitable Futures." *Global Scientific Journal, 13*(4), 1305–1345.
Matlin, S., et al. (2025). "Artificial Intelligence in Migrant Health: A Critical Perspective on Opportunities and Risks." *The Lancet Regional Health – Europe*, 57.
Mohla, S., et al. (2024). "Thinking Beyond Bias: Analyzing Multifaceted Impacts and Implications of AI on Gendered Labour." arXiv:2406.16207v1 [cs.CY]. Accessed December 31, 2025. <https://arxiv.org/pdf/2406.16207>.
Najibi, A. (2020). *Racial Discrimination in Face Recognition Technology*. Accessed December 31, 2025. <https://sciencepolicy.hsites.harvard.edu/blog/racial-discrimination-face-recognition-technology>.
Pal, S., et al. (2024). *AI's Missing Link: The Gender Gap in the Talent Pool*. Accessed December 31, 2025. <https://www.interface-eu.org/publications/ai-gender-gap>.
Pacian, J., et al. (2012). "Dyskryminacja bezpośrednia i pośrednia jako problem prawny i społeczny" [Direct and indirect discrimination as a legal and social problem]. *Roczniki Nauk Prawnych, 22*(3), 79–92.
Pizzinelli, C., et al. (2023). "Labor Market Exposure to AI: Cross-country Differences and Distributional Implications." *IMF Working Papers*, (216).
Pozzi, F., et al. (2025). *AI's Impact on Europe's Job Market: A Call for a Social Compact*. Accessed December 31, 2025. <https://www.epc.eu/publication/ais-impact-on-europes-job-market-a-call-for-a-social-compact/>.
de Oliveira Andrade, R. (2019). *Women resuming a prominent role in computing.* Accessed December 31, 2025. <https://revistapesquisa.fapesp.br/en/women-resuming-a-prominent-role-in-computing/>.
Shams, R. A., et al. (2025). "AI and the Quest for Diversity and Inclusion: A Systematic Literature Review." *AI Ethics*, 5, 411–438.
The Alan Turing Institute (2021). *Where Are the Women? Mapping the Gender Job Gap in AI*. Accessed December 31, 2025. <https://www.turing.ac.uk/news/where-are-women-mapping-gender-job-gap-ai>.
Tracey, D., et al. (2025). *AI Bias in Hiring: Algorithmic Recruiting and Your Rights*. Accessed December 31, 2025. <https://sanfordheisler.com/blog/2025/12/ai-bias-in-hiring-algorithmic-recruiting-and-your-rights/>.
Troszyński, M., et al. (2025). *Raport badawczy. Generatywna sztuczna inteligencja a polski rynek pracy* [Research Report: Generative Artificial Intelligence and the Polish Labor Market]. Warszawa: NASK – Państwowy Instytut Badawczy.
Williams, C., & Dencik, L. (2025). *AI Inequalities: Ethnicity*. Accessed December 31, 2025. <https://www.tuc.org.uk/blogs/wales/ai-inequalities-ethnicity>.

Algorithms, security, and civil defence

Krzysztof Kaczmarek[1], *Natalia Moch*[2],
Małgorzata Żmigrodzka[3], *Dorota Sylwia Majewicz*[4]

ABSTRACT
The growing presence of algorithms in public administration, national security systems, and crisis-management processes is profoundly transforming the concept of civil defence. Algorithmic decision-making increasingly shapes the allocation of resources, early warning mechanisms, and the coordination of civilian and military responses. This paper examines the strategic and social implications of algorithmic governance in the domains of security and civil protection. It discusses the dual nature of algorithms as both instruments of resilience and potential sources of systemic vulnerability. Particular attention is devoted to the ethical and institutional dimensions of algorithmic control, including transparency, accountability, and public trust. The analysis also considers the role of civil society and local communities in shaping adaptive and secure responses to algorithmic risks. The paper aims to contribute to a deeper understanding of how digital automation is reshaping the strategic architecture of civil defence in contemporary societies.

Keywords: Algorithms, security, civil defence, resilience, digital governance

Introduction

To say that digitalisation is transforming every aspect of how individuals, societies and states function is almost a truism. This is particularly true in the field of security, where algorithm-based digital tools play an increasingly important

1 Koszalin University of Technology in Koszalin, Faculty of Humanities
ORCID: <https://orcid.org/0–1-8519-1667>
Corresponding author's email: krzysztof.kaczmarek@tu.koszalin.pl

2 Military University of Technology in Warsaw, Faculty of Security, Logistics and Management
ORCID: <https://orcid.org/0–3-2177-0883>
Email: natalia.moch@wat.edu.pl

3 Polish Air Force University in Dęblin, Faculty of Safety Aviation
ORCID: <https://orcid.org/0–3-3896-0819>
email: m.zmigrodzka@law.mil.pl

4 Koszalin University of Technology in Koszalin, Faculty of Humanities
ORCID: <https://orcid.org/0–3-4568-3549>
email: dorota.majewicz@tu.koszalin.pl

role both in data analysis and in decision-support systems. Automated, real-time information processing enables faster responses to threats, but at the same time raises questions about the reliability, transparency and accountability of decisions made by machines or with their involvement. These changes are not merely technical; they effectively reshape the entire logic of civil defence and civil protection, which must now operate in an environment dependent on the functioning of information systems.

In practice, this means that traditional forms of planning for and responding to crisis situations must take into account the presence of new tools – from predictive models to self-learning artificial intelligence (AI). Algorithms analyse data from environmental sensors, monitoring systems and communication networks, allowing potential threats to be detected at an earlier stage (Malec, 2024, p. 23). Examples include systems for early warning against floods, fires, chemical contamination and cyberattacks. In some cases, AI also assists in coordinating the activities of emergency services by structuring and prioritising information incoming from different sources (Ganczar, 2023, p. 301).

The benefits of such solutions are evident – they shorten response times and help to limit losses. However, the associated challenges and risks cannot be ignored. Automation may lead to errors resulting from incorrect input data, excessive trust in algorithmic output or the phenomenon of so-called algorithmic bias (Kordzadeh & Ghasemaghaei, 2022, p. 391). Questions of responsibility also arise: who is accountable for the consequences of decisions made by a system that operates according to its own model? In civil defence, where time is critical but so is public trust, such doubts become particularly significant. The issue of data security is equally important – both with respect to the data used by these systems and to the data generated by them in the course of operation.

In the literature, the notion of digital resilience appears with increasing frequency, understood as the capacity of state institutions, society and technological systems to maintain continuity of functioning in a changing digital security environment (Boh et al., 2023, p. 344). Digital Europe, in turn, indicates that digital resilience refers to a society's ability to use digital technologies to prevent crises such as pandemics, natural disasters, cyberattacks and hybrid wars, and to confront them while preserving existing financial resources and security (Digital Europe, 2023, p. 6).

Civil defence in the digital age requires not only modern information systems, but also appropriate legal frameworks, staff competencies and citizens' trust in how the state uses data and in how "security" and "threat" are framed in public debate (Majewicz, 2025). For this reason, the digitalisation of security-related domains should be understood as a strategic task that interlinks technological, organisational, ethical and social dimensions.

The aim of this article is to present and analyse selected aspects of the algorithmisation of state security, with particular emphasis on civil defence and crisis management. Today, understanding the relationship between the algorithmisation of security and digital resilience constitutes one of the key conditions for the effective functioning of the state in an era of technological transformation. Reflection on these interdependencies is indispensable for designing modern models of civil defence and crisis management that are capable of meeting contemporary challenges.

The potential of artificial intelligence in civil protection and civil defence

Artificial intelligence and digitalisation play an increasingly important role in addressing crisis situations of diverse character – from pandemics, through threats caused by natural forces (e.g. storms, heavy rainfall, floods), to cyber-attacks. In a context where threats may arise suddenly, it is crucial to have effective tools for managing response activities and resolving crises swiftly. For this reason, AI-based solutions can be applied across different areas of civil protection and civil defence, aligning with all phases of crisis management – from prevention and preparedness, through response, to recovery (Comes, 2024, p. 6). Particularly useful in this regard are solutions that enable the rapid processing of vast amounts of data originating from sensors, monitoring systems, satellite imagery or social media (for instance, information posted by direct participants in a crisis situation). It should be noted that the data used by AI are heterogeneous in nature. They include contextual data (e.g. demographic or climatic data), data concerning the impact of a given threat (e.g. images, monitoring outputs) and data on human reactions to danger (e.g. mobility data, information from social media). Their use makes it possible to analyse a situation rapidly – often in real time, allowing for the early detection of symptoms of an impending crisis – and thus to take quick decisions on necessary actions, with a reduced margin of error. The modelling of scenario development by AI algorithms, in turn, facilitates the elaboration of different courses of action for the authorities and entities responsible for civil protection.

The solutions currently in use suggest that predictive algorithms will analyse data in a more precise and impartial manner than humans, anticipating the complex development of a given crisis situation. The outputs generated by these algorithms may also offer additional advantages, such as consistency, impartiality and objectivity in the assessment of available information. A clear risk in this regard, however, is the feeding of incomplete or biased data into the system, which will adversely affect the objectivity of the outputs and the accuracy of situational assessment (Habbal, Ali & Abuzaraida, 2024, p. 2).

Another benefit of using artificial intelligence algorithms in crisis management is cost reduction and improved operational efficiency through the elimination of repetitive tasks (Vladu, 2023, pp. 104–105). In traditional crisis-management models, a substantial portion of human and financial resources was devoted to processes such as data analysis, verification of information originating from multiple sources, and coordination of the activities of services, inspectorates and units involved in response. With the deployment of machine-learning algorithms and systems that automate information flows, it becomes possible to delegate these tasks to information systems, which perform them more quickly, with greater accuracy and without the risk of human error.

The automation of decision-making processes, in turn, enables a more efficient use of resources – both human and material – by allowing specialists to focus on strategic and analytical activities. For example, AI-based systems can independently classify emergency calls, analyse geolocation data or predict the evolution of a crisis situation in real time. Such solutions not only shorten response times but also reduce operational costs associated with maintaining large teams of analysts and operators. Moreover, AI algorithms can support logistics processes, the management of civil protection stocks and the optimisation of evacuation routes, thereby enhancing the effectiveness of action in emergency situations. This is of particular importance in the context of civil protection and civil defence.

Cybersecurity and system resilience in crisis management

The functioning of automated systems is closely dependent on the stability of electricity supply, as even short interruptions can disrupt their operation and cause a loss of process continuity (Kaczmarek & Cholewińska, 2024, p. 92). Disturbances in power supply may at times paralyse multiple interlinked systems, including those servicing critical infrastructure and public administration (Karpiuk, Pizło & Kaczmarek, 2023, p. 647). In such a context, cybersecurity acquires particular importance, as not only the stability of information networks but also the resilience of the entire crisis-management system depends on it. Its current level may still give rise to justified concern (Moch & Wereda, 2024, p. 1328). These concerns primarily stem from the growing complexity and frequency of cyber threats, which increasingly take the form of hybrid attacks directed at elements of the state's critical infrastructure.

In many cases, the ICT systems used in public administration and the energy sector are based on outdated technological solutions, which limits their capacity to respond effectively to incidents in real time. An additional problem lies in the dispersion of institutional responsibility and the absence of full interoperability between entities responsible for cybersecurity, which hampers the coordination of actions in crisis situations. Insufficient human resources and the inadequate level of automation of security processes further deepen this gap, increasing the risk of disruptions in the functioning of systems that are of strategic importance to the state.

In response to the shortcomings identified above, the concept of digital resilience is gaining in importance, understood as the capacity of information systems to maintain key operational functions despite disruptions, failures or cyberattacks. In the context of accelerated digitalisation, resilience to shocks is increasingly linked to the effective use of ICT systems – from deploying data analytics and artificial intelligence to facilitate early interventions in crisis situations, to implementing digital social innovations aimed at providing immediate assistance to marginalised communities. The use of AI in post-disruption recovery is also of critical significance (Tim & Leidner, 2023, p. 1184). Digital resilience encompasses both technological and organisational dimensions, including infrastructure redundancy, the ability to restore data rapidly, and staff competencies in crisis response. The literature emphasises that building digital resilience does not consist solely in strengthening security measures, but above all in developing flexible adaptive mechanisms that allow systems to maintain continuity of operation under conditions of uncertainty (Vert, Sharpanskykh & Curran, 2021). This approach constitutes a key component of contemporary crisis management, in which the algorithmisation of processes and the deployment of artificial intelligence can significantly enhance the state's capacity to respond to and recover from incidents that disrupt the functioning of critical infrastructure.

Algorithms in crisis management and civil defence

The development of digital technologies and artificial intelligence has introduced a new dimension of decision automation into the realm of public security. Algorithms – understood as sets of rules that enable data processing and partially autonomous decision-making – have become a key tool supporting crisis management and civil defence. Contemporary security systems employ machine learning to analyse data from environmental sensors, video surveillance and critical infrastructure, which makes it possible to detect threats earlier and better forecast the consequences of natural disasters, technical failures or terrorist acts (Binns, 2018).

In practice, algorithms are currently used, among other things, to prioritise resources in rescue operations, optimise evacuation routes and coordinate activities between civilian and military services. For instance, predictive models used in spatial analysis make it possible to identify areas with the highest risk of human or material losses, which significantly increases the effectiveness of response in the first hours following a crisis event (Helbing et al., 2021).

At the same time, algorithms are gaining importance in shaping public policies in the fields of security and societal resilience. Many states are introducing data-driven risk assessment systems that support decisions concerning the allocation of resources and the management of personnel and infrastructure (OECD, 2022). Such solutions contribute to improving institutional efficiency, yet they may also lead to a reduction in the transparency of decision-making processes and to the blurring of boundaries between technological control and political accountability (Pasquale, 2015).

Contemporary security systems operate in an environment of constant inflows of information from multiple sources – ranging from environmental sensors and monitoring systems to the media and social communication. The volume of data collected is growing exponentially, which on the one hand enhances the analytical potential of public administration, while on the other makes it more difficult to select information that is genuinely relevant. In practice, this means that not all data entering decision-making systems possess the same epistemic value. Paradoxically, the absence of certain data is at times less risky than their excess, as it compels more cautious calculation and more deliberate planning of actions. For algorithm-based systems, this implies not so much the need to accumulate ever larger datasets as the need to refine methods of data processing and to critically assess data quality (Ficoń & Sokołowski, 2023, pp. 488–489).

With the growing use of AI tools and machine learning in data analysis, a new type of risk emerges. It concerns not only the quality of the information entering the systems, but also the way in which algorithms learn and process incoming data. Machine-learning models are sensitive to errors in training datasets, which may contain incomplete, one-sided or distorted data. In such cases, the algorithm may replicate and reinforce the same errors in its forecasts and decisions.

The danger also lies in the fact that these errors often remain invisible until the system begins to operate under real-world conditions. It then becomes apparent that the model performs well in situations it has encountered during the training phase, but fails in new, non-standard circumstances. Such excessive fitting to the training data, known as overfitting, may lead to erroneous risk assessments, inadequate decisions or unjustified alerts (Roth et al., 2025, p. 35).

One of the more advanced and, at the same time, more dangerous – because often imperceptible – threats associated with artificial intelligence are so-called data poisoning attacks, that is, deliberate attacks consisting in introducing erroneous, manipulated or misleading data into training sets. The aim of such activity is to disrupt the machine-learning process and cause the model to respond in certain situations in an incorrect way, or in a way that is predictable from the attacker's perspective. Poisoned data may constitute only a small fraction of the entire training set, yet its impact on the model can be significant, especially in systems where the training process is automated and takes place without human supervision (Jagielski et al., 2018).

In practice, such attacks are divided into several basic types. The first are label-flipping attacks, which involve intentionally altering the labels of training data – for example, assigning correct images to incorrect categories. As a result, the model learns erroneous relationships, leading to misclassifications at the deployment stage (Akram et al., 2024, p. 2168). The second category consists of clean-label backdoor attacks, in which the attacker introduces into the data a specific, often imperceptible pattern (trigger pattern). The model functions correctly in most cases, but in the presence of this pattern it reacts in a completely different way – which, in a security context, may mean, for instance, overlooking a particular type of threat or misinterpreting input data (Zhao et al., 2024). A more advanced form is gradient poisoning attacks, which occur in federated learning environments where training data originate from multiple distributed sources. In this case, the attack consists in manipulating the gradients of the model, that is, the parameters responsible for the learning process (Bouaziz et al., 2024).

Such interference is particularly dangerous in systems used in public security and crisis management. It may lead to erroneous situational assessments, incorrect allocation of resources or a failure to respond to genuine threats. For this reason, protection against data poisoning attacks requires continuous monitoring of data quality, the use of model validation and auditing methods, and the inclusion of humans in the oversight of AI systems (human-in-the-loop oversight). At the same time, it should be noted that intentional interference in AI training processes may form part of hybrid operations.

Ethical and institutional challenges

The use of algorithms in security systems raises fundamental ethical and institutional questions. Decisions based on data and predictive models often have a direct impact on citizens' lives, and the lack of full transparency in the operation of these systems may lead to an erosion of public trust (Floridi & Cowls, 2019). The key challenges concern responsibility, transparency and oversight with regard to algorithmic decision-making processes.

Firstly, AI-based systems may reinforce existing biases and inequalities if input data reflect skewed social or historical patterns (Eubanks, 2018). In the security context, this implies a risk of unfair treatment of particular social groups, regions or local communities in the allocation of resources or the organisation of evacuations.

Secondly, the absence of mechanisms for auditing and controlling algorithms may give rise to so-called "black boxes," in which the decision-making process becomes opaque even to the creators of the system (Burrell, 2016).

In public administration, this constitutes a serious threat to the principles of democratic accountability and the rule of law. Consequently, there is a growing emphasis on the need to implement ethical principles in the design and deployment of algorithms, such as fairness, accountability and transparency (FAT) (Jobin, Ienca and Vayena, 2019).

Thirdly, there is a need to develop institutional frameworks that enable the control and certification of algorithmic systems used in civil defence. The European Union Aviation Safety Agency (EASA) and the European Commission indicate in strategic documents that every AI-based system in the field of public security should be subject to an independent risk assessment and a mandatory registration requirement (EASA, 2023).

Public trust is one of the most important factors conditioning the effectiveness of technology-based security systems. The implementation of algorithms in crisis management requires not only technical competencies, but also social consent and legitimacy. Public opinion research indicates that acceptance of decision automation in public administration increases when citizens have access to information on how the system operates and feel that they can participate in the process of its evaluation (Power BI Report, 2024).

Civil society and local communities play a dual role in this regard. On the one hand, they constitute a source of information and social indicators that can be incorporated into the databases of predictive systems; on the other, they perform a controlling function, providing democratic oversight over technological instruments of power (Jasanoff, 2003). Their engagement strengthens social resilience by co-creating a culture of responsibility and transparency.

Building trust therefore requires openness on the part of state institutions and the implementation of principles of public explainability, i.e. the capacity to explain to citizens how and why particular algorithmic decisions have been made (Krauze-Maślankowska & Majewicz, 2025). Only under such conditions is it possible to reconcile technological efficiency with the requirements of democracy and public ethics.

Conclusions and recommendations

The use of algorithms for the purposes of civil defence may have both positive and negative effects on security. In this context, it is crucial to understand the challenges associated with the application of artificial intelligence. Equally important, however, is harnessing its potential in processes related to data collection, analysis and reporting. The complexity of the algorithms employed by AI generates new risks. A key issue will be the level of trust in AI systems, particularly in the acceptance and implementation of new technologies. Individuals will be more inclined to use and rely on such systems when they perceive them as reliable. It also appears that, at the current stage of development, AI systems deployed for civil protection and civil defence should incorporate human oversight. It is essential, after all, to use AI algorithms in a responsible manner.

Bibliography

Akram, J., Anaissi, A., Akram, A., Singh Rathore, R., & Jhaveri, R. H. (2024). "Adversarial Label-Flipping Attack and Defense for Anomaly Detection in Spatial Crowdsourcing UAV Services," *IEEE Transactions on Consumer Electronics*, 1, 2163–2174. <https://doi.org/10.1109/TCE.2024.3448541>.

Binns, R. (2018). "Algorithmic Accountability and Public Reason," *Philosophy & Technology*, 31, 543–556. <https://doi.org/10.1007/s13347-017-0263-5>.

Boh, W., Constantinides, P., Padmanabhan, B., & Viswanathan, S. (2023). "Building digital resilience against major shocks," *MIS Quarterly*, 1, 343–360.

Bouaziz, W., El-Mhamdi, E.-M., & Usunier, N. (2024). "Inverting Gradient Attacks Makes Powerful Data Poisoning," arXiv preprint arXiv:2410.21453. <https://doi.org/10.48550/arXiv.2410.21453>.

Burrell, J. (2016). "How the Machine 'Thinks': Understanding Opacity in Machine Learning Algorithms," *Big Data & Society, 1*, 1–12. <https://doi.org/10.1177/2053951715622512>.

Comes, T. (2024). "AI for Crisis Decisions," *Ethics and Information Technology, 26*(12), 1–14. <http://doi.org/10.1007/s10676-024-09750-0>.

Digital Europe (2023). *The Digital frontline: 15 Actions to Boost Europe's Digital Resilience*. <https://digital-europe-website-v1.s3.fr-par.scw.cloud/uploads/2023/03/DIGITALEUROPE-TECHNOLOGY-IN-THE-FACE-OF-HYBRID-THREATS-FINAL-WEB-1.pdf>.

EASA (2023). *AI Roadmap 2.0: Toward Trustworthiness in Aviation Systems.* European Union Aviation Safety Agency.

Eubanks, V. (2018). *Automating Inequality: How High-tech Tools Profile, Police, and Punish the Poor.* New York: Picador, St Martin's Press.

Ficoń, K., & Sokołowski, W. (2023). "Wykorzystanie komputerowych metod eksploracji danych i odkrywania wiedzy w zarządzaniu kryzysowym," *Rocznik Bezpieczeństwa Morskiego*, 17, 483–506.

Floridi, L., & Cowls, J. (2019). "A Unified Framework of Five Principles for AI in Society," *Harvard Data Science Review*, 1. <https://doi.org/10.1162/99608f92.8cd550d1>.

Ganczar, M. (2023). "Wykorzystanie sztucznej inteligencji w ochronie środowiska," *Gdańskie Studia Prawnicze*, 4, 294–307. <https://doi.org/10.26881/gsp.2023.4.18>.

Habbal, A., Ali, M. K., & Abuzaraida, M. A. (2024). "Artificial Intelligence Trust, Risk and Security Management (AI TRiSM): Frameworks, Applications, Challenges and Future Research Directions," *Expert Systems With Applications*, 240, 1–14. <http://doi.org/10.1016/j.eswa.2023.122442>.

Helbing, D., et al. (2021). "Will Democracy Survive Big Data and Artificial Intelligence?" In D. Helbing (Ed.), *Towards Digital Enlightenment. Zürich: Springer*, pp. 73–98. <https://doi.org/10.1007/978-3-319-90869-4_7>.

Jagielski, M., Oprea, A., Biggio, B., Liu, C., Nita-Rotaru, C., & Li, B. (2018). "Manipulating Machine Learning: Poisoning Attacks and Countermeasures for Regression Learning," IEEE Symposium on Security and Privacy (SP). <https://doi.org/10.48550/arXiv.1804.00308>.

Jasanoff, S. (2003). "Technologies of Humility: Citizen Participation in Governing Science," *Minerva* 41, 223–244 (2003). <https://doi.org/10.1023/A:1025557512320>.

Jobin, A., Ienca, M., & Vayena, E. (2019). "The Global Landscape of AI Ethics Guidelines," *Nature Machine Intelligence*, 1, 389–399. <https://doi.org/10.1038/s42256-019-0088-2>.

Kaczmarek, K., & Cholewińska, D. (2024). "Security and Hybrid Threats," *Przegląd Nauk o Obronności*, 20, 91–100. <https://doi.org/10.37055/pno/208458>.

Karpiuk, M., Pizło, W., & Kaczmarek, K. (2023). "Cybersecurity Management–Current State and Directions of Change," *International Journal of Legal Studies (IJOLS)*, 2, 645–663. <https://doi.org/10.5604/01.3001.0054.2880>.

Kordzadeh, N., & Ghasemaghaei, M. (2022). "Algorithmic Bias: Review, Synthesis, and Future Research Directions," *European Journal of Information Systems*, 3, 388–409. <https://doi.org/10.1080/0960085X.2021.1927212>.

Krauze-Maślankowska, P., & Majewicz, D. S. (2025). "Cybersecurity in the Development of Smart Cities: A Big Data Analysis of Digital Security Management Practices by Local Public Administration in Poland," *Ius et Securitas*, 2, 55–66.

Majewicz, D. S. (2025). "Linguistic Nuances in Crisis Communication: Advancing Conflict Mediation and Defense Education in Poland," *Myśl Strategiczna*, 2, 44–57.

Malec, N. (2024). "Sztuczna inteligencja a bezpieczeństwo państwa," *Prawo i Bezpieczeństwo*, 1, 20–24.

Moch, N., & Wereda, W. (2024). "Management of Urban Security and New Technologies," *European Research Studies Journal*, 4, 1318–1331.

OECD (2022). *AI in the Public Sector: Building Trust and Ensuring Accountability*. Paris: OECD Publishing.

Pasquale, F. (2015). *The Black Box Society: The Secret Algorithms that Control Money and Information*. Cambridge: Harvard University Press.

Power BI Report (2024). Perception of Algorithmic Governance in Public Administration. Internal survey dataset.

Roth, B., de Araujo, P. H. L., Xia, Y., Kaltenbrunner, S., & Korab, C. (2025). "Specification Overfitting in Artificial Intelligence," *Artificial Intelligence Review*, 58, 1–37. <https://doi.org/10.1007/s10462-024-11040-6>.

Tim, Yenni and Leidner, Dorothy E. (2023) "Digital Resilience: A Conceptual Framework for Information Systems Research," *Journal of the Association for Information Systems, 24*(5), 1184-1198. DOI: 10.17705/1jais.00842

Vert, M., Sharpanskykh, A., & Curran, R. (2021). "Adaptive Resilience of Complex Safety-Critical Sociotechnical Systems: Toward a Unified Conceptual Framework and Its Formalization," *Sustainability*, 13, 1–23. <https://doi.org/10.3390/su132413915>.

Vladu, O.-M. (2023). "Digital Transformation in Crisis Management: The Key Role of Artificial Intelligence," *Scientific Research and Education in the Air Force*, 103–110. <http://doi.org/10.19062/2247-3173.2023.24.15>.

Zhao, S., Luu, A. T., Fu, J., Wen, J., & Luo, W. (2024). "Exploring Clean Label Backdoor Attacks and Defense in Language Models," *IEEE/ACM Transactions on Audio, Speech, and Language Processing*, 32. <https://doi.org/10.1109/TASLP.2024.3407571>.

Reworking the local public sector? Mapping research trends and challenges related to the new technologies

Ewa Włodyka[1]

ABSTRACT
This article examines how research on new technologies, artificial intelligence (AI), and digitalisation, are addresses to local government, local administration, and local public services within the broader discourse on the Future of Work. Using an exploratory bibliometric and qualitative approach, the study preliminarily, without complexity, analyses publications from 2020 to 2025 indexed in six major academic databases (Scopus, SAGE Journals, Google Scholar, Academia.edu, EBSCO, and Springer), applying three sets of keyword combinations linking technological change with local-level governance and services. The findings demonstrate a growing and diversified body of literature, predominantly focused on strategic and managerial dimensions of local government, such as city governance, urban mobility, environmental monitoring, and digital communication with citizens. Qualitative analysis indicates that AI-based tools-such as predictive analytics and chatbots-can enhance efficiency, resource allocation, and proactive problem-solving in local governance, thereby partially confirming the hypothesis that new technologies improve the quality of local public services. At the same time, these benefits are shown to be conditional and uneven, constrained by challenges related to data protection, ethical governance, organisational readiness, and cybersecurity. This study is trying to reveals gaps in the literature, including the limited attention paid to local administration as an executive structure. Moreover, digital exclusion-particularly behavioural and socio-economic barriers to access-remains markedly underexplored despite its implications for equality, democratic legitimacy, and citizen participation. The article identifies four key areas requiring further research: the labour-related consequences of digital transformation, changing employment models and skill requirements in local government, digital exclusion as a governance challenge, and the impact of AI on the legitimacy, accountability, and transparency of public decision-making. Overall, the study maps current research trends while highlighting the need for more integrated, citizen-oriented, and employment-sensitive approaches to understanding how new technologies are reshaping the local public sector.

Keywords: Future of work, local government, new technologies, artificial intelligence, public administration

Introduction

Historically, technology has driven economic growth and transformed jobs (Arias et al., 2025; *Emerging Technologies and the Future of Work in*

---

[1] Koszalin University of Technology

Europe / Digital Skills and Jobs Platform, n.d.; Kolade & Owoseni, 2022). The development of the global knowledge society and the rapid integration of Information and Communication Technologies (ICT)[2] make it imperative to acquire digital skills necessary for employment and participation in society. Attention is drawn to creativity (Cropley, 2020), the professionalism of teaching (Akgunduz & Mesutoglu, 2021) and the role of new technologies and the decreasing scope of routine work (Goos et al., 2014). A public sector employer in local government is seeking employees with digital skills (E. Włodyka, 2021). This topic was already being discussed before the spread of Open AI and just before it, with the focus, as is often the case with European values, on the human being (European Commission. Directorate General for Research and Innovation., 2018, 2021). New technologies are changing not only the functioning of public administration through digitalisation, but also societies in terms of opportunities and threats to civil society (Niesporek, 2025). This is all the more important as new technologies can become an element of the development of civic participation (Kapsa & Musiał-Karg, 2020; Lubik-Reczek et al., 2020; Podgórska-Rykała & Pospieszna, 2024) or pro-democratic transformations. It has become commonplace for non-democratic regimes to integrate information and communication technologies (ICTs) into their governance system, make use of these new digital opportunities in an authoritarian setting remains understudied. Rabe et al., (2026) find that a surprisingly large share of Chinese citizens engages with the new ICT-based participatory venues. While citizens seem to be quite aware of the risks of using ICTs, such as data security breaches or digital surveillance, these do not seem to hamper participation (Rabe et al., 2025). The link between institutions responsible for law-making and entities from the economic sector is also highlighted (Mehdi & Naz, 2025). AI should not be confined solely to the domain of exact sciences but should also be deepened from a multidisciplinary perspective, encompassing the humanities and social sciences.

It seems truistic to say that local governments need to manage resources more effectively, provide public services more efficiently and engage residents in decision-making processes (Smalec et al., 2025, p. 497). The local

---

2 ICT is a collective term for all technologies used to collect, process, transmit and share information, whether in text, voice, visual or multimedia form.

and regional levels of government are on the frontline of the introduction of new digital technologies and processes in public services: although central governments play a leading role in the decision to launch and roll out digitalisation programmes and initiatives, most public services are delivered at municipal, local, or regional government level. Governments at all levels are looking for new and innovative ways to include individuals in vulnerable situations such as youth, migrants, persons with disabilities and families facing multiple challenges, in the labour market and in society more generally (OECD, 2023). But still the technological revolution meets emerging issues and challenges. On the other side, there are also concerns that new technologies solutions are a Trojan horse, exploiting the lack of technical knowledge at public agencies and shifting decision-making power from public agencies to market parties, thereby undermining digital sovereignty and public values (Bharosa, 2022).

It is also important to remember the significant role played by local government units in state policy and the life of local communities (Czuryk et al., 2015; Dolnicki (ed.), 2023; Izdebski, 2020). All the more so, local public administration, as a public sector employer, is burdened with the responsibility of implementing new technologies in the organisation of civil servants' work, the management of the most frequently transferred data of citizens, and communication with them and external stakeholders. Does this mean that public administration must adapt to new conditions and follow the implementation used in the private sector? Such a marriage has not always proved effective in history. I am referring here to New Public Management as a style of public management that implements solutions designed for the private sector as described for example by Lane, Reiter and Klenk (Lane, 2002; Reiter & Klenk, 2019).

Methodology

In view of the centrality of technology diffusion in fostering local innovations and economic development in developing countries, it is surprising that our understanding of the challenges and opportunities in scaling-up technologies remains limited (Amankwah-Amoah, 2019). Some regions face specific challenges related, among other things, to political culture and the implementation of new technologies in the public sector (Chumaceiro

Hernández et al., 2025)[3]. This further confirms the need for interdisciplinary research not only on the functioning of local and regional administration, but also on the development of civil society through new forms of political communication and civic participation. This is already happening, as can be seen from the quantity (without loss of quality) of research in this area. Here are some examples of research conducted on: local government, local communities, public administration at local and regional level, using new technologies, artificial intelligence and digitalisation in public services. This article combines quantitative and qualitative research, using secondary data analysis and a case study.

The purpose of this study is to conduct a preliminary quantitative and qualitative analysis (within a selected scope) of data on new technologies (including digitisation and the use of artificial intelligence) in public administration at the level of local government units and local public services in the period 2020–2025 for data published in selected research databases. The use of selected keywords by the authors of the studies was taken as the variable. Keywords in quantitative research were selected based on their relevance to both technological and administrative domains, combining terms such as "new technologies," "AI," and "digitalisation" with institutional markers like "local government," "local administration," and "local services." Searches were conducted across six major academic databases (Scopus, SAGE Journals, Google Scholar, Academia.edu, EBSCO, and Springer) on 12 December 2025. While the quantitative dimension of the study relies on the assumption that higher frequencies of keyword combinations reflect stronger scholarly engagement, several methodological limitations were acknowledged, including variations in search algorithms across databases, potential duplication of results, and the lack of content-based validation. The interpretation of data was guided by identifying thematic gaps and dominant research foci, revealing an emphasis on institutional and strategic levels over operational and service-level concerns. The qualitative component draws on secondary literature and case studies to contextualise the findings, suggesting both the

[3] Like in sub-Saharan Africa – there the study identified a host of factors such as weak regulatory enforcement systems, lack of financial credit availability, and limited banking services, which have created conditions for technological innovations such as mobile phone-based banking, mPedigree, "cardiopad" and M-PEPEA to emerge.

maturity of the topic and areas requiring deeper empirical investigation, particularly in relation to employment models, competencies in the public sector, and ethical governance in the age of AI.

The methodology adopted in this study follows an exploratory-descriptive and bibliometric approach, grounded in the theoretical framework of evidence mapping and informed by principles of science and technology studies as applied to public administration. The aim was to map the presence and distribution of research related to digital transformation-encompassing ICT, artificial intelligence, and digitalisation, in the context of local government, local administration, and local public services.

Although the cited studies are not geographically limited to Europe, one aspect should be emphasised. While Asian countries are leading the way in the implementation of technological solutions in state management and, through this, the provision of public services, Europe is the leader in terms of regulation and the creation of a legal system and framework for the safe and transparent use of technology in the public sector. After all, the European Union's priority goal over the last ten years of the twenty-first century has been to create a smarter Europe by supporting digital social and economic transformation and making full use of information and communication technologies. Current EU strategic documents also show that the implementation of Europe's digital transformation and the regulation of AI remain, alongside the ecological transformation, the most important challenge for the EU (European Commission, 2022b, 2022a). The implementation of the EU's digital transformation policy is expected to lead, among other things, to the digital transformation of public services. The digital modernisation of public services assumes that by the end of 2030, 100 % of the most important public services will be provided online to EU citizens and businesses; 100 % of EU citizens will have access to medical records (electronic registers); 80 % of citizens will be able to use digital identity solutions. The digital transformation of European public administration is of paramount importance for the European economy and society (Dudzik, 2021, p. 8), including at local and regional level.

The analysis of the studies was conducted based on their scope: international, national or local (including case studies). In addition, the levels were divided into research topics, with an attempt to determine whether any of the scope levels focused on a selected topic. Desk research was used, taking into account the achievements of researchers from leading scientific associations in the field of political science and administration[4]. The time period selected was from 2020, when the digitisation of many public services was forced, in a sense, by the emergence of the COVID-19 pandemic and the associated restrictions. At the same time, two years later, in November 2022, the first widely used generative artificial intelligence model from the Large Language Models group, ChatGPT from OpenAI, was released for general use. The past two years have marked an explosion of interest in public sector adoption of artificial intelligence (AI) technologies. Governments nationwide are increasingly procuring enterprise AI solutions, such as decision-support tools, resident-facing chatbots, and smart cities technologies, to automate bureaucratic processes (P. Silva et al., 2019, p. 4). From that moment on, some countries considered implementing even broader AI solutions at the central level of state management (either comprehensively or through selected institutions or ministries) (E. M. Włodyka, n.d.). Already at this stage, divergent approaches to the issues are noticeable, ranging from the United States' emphasis on the "innovation gap" to the European Union's "trust deficit" and China's "stability risk," and consequently different regulatory policies (Mark & Morison, 2025). Critical questions are also arising about the future direction and resilience of "algorithmic decision-making" governance, going beyond the administrative, political and legal aspects of the issue and entering the realm of ethics, security and psychology.

Almost all major economies in the world have national strategies for the development of AI, and many of them are investing in the development of their own sovereign national models of generative artificial intelligence (for various reasons), such as China, Poland, France and Germany (Singh & Sengupta, 2025; Tjondronegoro, 2024; Wang, 2025). The continuously improving capabilities of various AI-based systems have led to the use of AI in an increasing amount of politically significant settings (Sætra, 2021, p. 27). AI is now also used in official government decision-making processes and even more[5] and the issue

---

[4] An additional difficulty here is the lack of a uniform methodology for dividing scientific disciplines and sub-disciplines, used not only by researchers from different countries, but also by repositories and research platforms that generate research papers.

[5] Albania made headlines around the world as the first country to appoint an artificial intelligence system as a government minister. On 11 September 2025, Prime Minister Edi Rama introduced Diella, a digital avatar of a woman in traditional Albanian dress, as Minister of State for Artificial Intelligence, responsible for overseeing public procurement.

of applying AI in public policies and public management using algorithms is a phenomenon that is being studied (De Fine Licht & De Fine Licht, 2020; De Fine Licht & Folland, 2025; Mahroof et al., 2025). Skaug Saetra in his research has examined the potential for AI in official political settings, distinguishing between five types of AI used to support, assist, alleviate, augment or supplant decision-makers. AI in politics has the potential to drastically change how politics is performed, and as politics entails answering some of society's most fundamental questions (P. Silva et al., 2019). AI algorithms require multiple forms of accountability to be trustworthy (Agbabiaka et al., 2025). But still a key challenge is the misalignment between ML models and the realities of public sector decision-making (Fischer-Abaigar et al., 2024).

Also, in public administration at the local and regional level, through local government in the provision of public services, there is a need to incorporate new technologies (including artificial intelligence) as an element that improves the quality of local public services (this is the hypothesis H1 of this article). Hence, the basic research question (RQ1) was derived: how is the issue of new technologies (including the use of artificial intelligence and digitisation policies) in local government and local public services researched? The auxiliary research question is: in which areas does artificial intelligence have a significant impact on the activities of local governments? The study is preliminary and non-comprehensive, taking into account only selected variables and research results.

Definitional and legal basis

AI is not a homogeneous concept, not only within related scientific disciplines but also in the normative acts of individual state actors on the international stage. As a scientific discipline, artificial intelligence encompasses several approaches and techniques, such as machine learning (with particular examples including deep learning and reinforcement learning), machine reasoning (which includes planning, scheduling, knowledge representation and reasoning, search, and optimisation), and robotics (which encompasses control, perception, sensors, as well as the integration of all other techniques with cyberphysical systems) (*A DEFINITION OF AI: MAIN CAPABILITIES AND DISCIPLINES. Definition Developed for the Purpose of the AI HLEG's Deliverables, EUROPEAN COMMISSION*, 2019). In the AI Act, the definition of AI is not limited to a single technological application but extends to all machine-based systems capable of adaptive behaviour that share the ability to generate outputs of various typologies following the processing of received inputs (*Regulation (EU) 2024/1689 of the European Parliament and of the Council of 13 June 2024 Laying down Harmonised Rules on Artificial Intelligence and Amending Regulations (EC) No 300/2008, (EU) No 167/2013, (EU) No 168/2013, (EU) 2018/858, (EU) 2018/1139 and (EU) 2019/2144 and Directives 2014/90/EU, (EU) 2016/797 and (EU) 2020/1828 (Artificial Intelligence Act) (Text with EEA Relevance) PE/24/2024/REV/1*, n.d.).

The empirical findings reveal that AI, particularly through the usage of big data derived from sensor networks, can play a central role in facilitating social innovation and data-based decision-making in future urban contexts. The results further demonstrate that social innovation mediates the relationship between AI and decision-making effectiveness, thereby strengthening governance efficiency. Conversely, internal IoT vulnerabilities were found to weaken this positive association, highlighting the need for robust cybersecurity measures. Overall, this study provides significant theoretical and practical implications for policymakers, urban planners, and scholars. It underscores the pivotal role of social innovation in integrating AI into the design of sustainable and resilient cities, while simultaneously emphasising the importance of addressing security and governance challenges stemming from IoT-related risks (Yang & Khalid, 2025). The EU itself, apart from regulating AI, is also exploring its potential alongside other ICT solutions. There is much potential for the fruitful exploitation of AI by the public sector. Although, to date, it is noted that AI is most widely employed at national level around Europe, exploitation of AI by local and regional authorities (LRAs, also known as subnational authorities) – as the closest level to citizens – is essential to foster the spreading and public acceptance of this technology (European Committee of the Regions. Commission for Economic Policy et al., 2024).

Role of artificial intelligence in local governments, mainly focus how smart technologies improve city management or, as well, communication with residents (Smalec et al., 2025, p. 497).

State of research – analysis

Most studies after 2020 are based on the verification of specific technological solutions. They fit into the trend of how smart technologies improve city management and communication. The search was narrowed down to publications from 2020 to 2025, mainly scientific articles (including review articles). However, the field and scientific disciplines were not narrowed down for the purposes of qualitative analysis.

Table 1: Results from repetitorium (database of scientific articles) and searched keywords

No.	Repetitorium (database of scientific articles)	Search keyword ("new technologies" OR "AI" OR "digitalisation") AND "local government"	("new technologies" OR "AI" OR "digitalisation") AND "local administration"	("new technologies" OR "AI" OR "digitalisation") AND "local services"
1	Scopus (Science Direct)[6]	20,734	2,012	158
2	Sage Journals[7]	3,864	350	322
3	Google scholar[8]	34,100	16,600	11,600
4	Academiaedu[9]	7	7	8
5	Ebsco (Political Science Complete)	354	33	14
6	Springer[10]	2,409	276	189

Source: own work based on searching the indicated databases and thematic keywords on 12 December 2025.

A quantitative analysis of publications for the specified phrases in selected databases was used. It was assumed that a larger number of results indicates existing scientific interest, the maturity of a given research topic and its potential for further qualitative and exploratory analysis. Even this rather selective and unrepresentative analysis of bibliometric data indicates that issues related to new technologies, artificial intelligence and digitisation in the

6 Review and research articles.
7 Articles.
8 Articles, chapters and books.
9 Articles.
10 Article, research article, review articles.

context of local government and public services are of clear interest in scientific literature. Most of the research concerns the strategic and organisational level of local government, rather than just administration as an executive structure or specific services. This may suggest that greater importance is attached to public management as a whole, including decision-making and planning, rather than just execution. The weaker results for the terms "local administration" and "local services" may indicate insufficient coverage of topics related to the daily practices of officials, the accessibility and quality of local public services and administration at the local level in the context of new technologies. At the same time, the importance of interdisciplinary research combining ICT, public policy, management, civic participation and digital ethics is growing.

The data indicates that the term "local government" is much more prevalent in the literature than "local administration." This may mean that research focuses more often on local government as a comprehensive power structure, political system and institution responsible for shaping local policies than on its executive (civil service) aspect and element of the central structure of public administration bodies in the state. The above comparison shows that research on the impact of new technologies on specific services may be insufficiently developed. This may indicate a research niche in the area of operationalising digital transformation at the level of service provision and its impact on the employment structure (e.g. automation of customer service, new competence profiles for local government employees).

Although this analysis is not comprehensive and does not take into account differences in the search engine methodologies of the databases used, it nevertheless creates space for in-depth quantitative analyses (including literature, systematic, scoping or bibliometric reviews).

Exploring AI's potentials to improve decision-making, streamline public services, and foster greater accountability and transparency in local governments is also the subject of systematic research by Harvard scientists (*Artificial Intelligence | Data-Smart City Solutions, n.d.)* They work in the emerging area of artificial intelligence and generative artificial intelligence (AI/GenAI) focuses on how cities can responsibly and effectively integrate AI/GenAI into governance and service delivery. They explore AI's potential to improve decision-making, streamline public services, and foster greater accountability and transparency in local governments.

The analysis of the research results deliberately omitted the issues of "smart city" and "smart village." However, this is a large area[11]. The omission is deliberate, although it impoverishes this analysis, but due to the significant search results, it deserves a separate, in-depth analysis. This is all the more so because when discussing the stages of evolution of the smart city idea from 1.0 to 4.0 (Ingwersen & Serrano-López, 2018; Kaiser, 2024; Tundys et al., 2022), the discourse on new technologies is mentioned not as an end in itself, but only as a tool for achieving sustainable development (Aditya et al., 2023; Alizadeh & Sharifi, 2023; Batty et al., 2012; Vieira et al., 2023).

Research – international scope

Scientific associations, as voluntary, self-governing associations of researchers whose aim is to organise and maintain a research community around a specific field of knowledge, are an important source for disseminating research results. Scientific associations play a key role in research, providing a platform for cooperation, knowledge exchange and the promotion of scientific achievements (Pietruch-Reizes, 2019).

Those on an international scale play an even more crucial role in the development of modern science, as they create lasting, transnational research communities that transcend the boundaries of national academic systems. They enable the exchange of theories, methods and research perspectives, promoting the internationalisation of research and improving its quality. In this sense, they are not only a tool for research collaboration, but also an important element of the global knowledge infrastructure. In this context, they are also a place where new technologies are harnessed as modern research tools. Are new technologies themselves becoming the subject of research interest among international communities of researchers on local government? In March 2025, a study initiated by the Comparative Studies on Local Government and Politics research group of researchers affiliated with the International Political Science Association began mapping scientific

[11] Search results in Scopus for the thematic term in the corresponding period of 2020–2025 yielded articles and scientific monographs on "smart city" **84,991** and 9,273 for "smart village," respectively.

research on local government and politics (Navarro & Cravacuore, 2025). It turned out that only 12.3 % of respondents among IPSA member researchers deal with the area of "Innovation and Digital Transformation" in their scientific work[12]. This was the penultimate item indicated by researchers.

Table 2: Selected topics by geographical area

		Research area indicated by researchers		
	Geographical area	**The research area LEAST interesting to researchers**	**Innovation and Digital Transformation (research percentage in a given geographical area)**	**The research area MOST interesting to researchers**
1	South America	*Crisis Management and Resilience* 1.7 %	4 %	*Public Policy at the Local Level* 20.1 %
2	Oceania	*Innovation and Digital Transformation* 0 %	0 %	*Governance Structures and Institutional* Design 22.7 %
3	North America	*Innovation and Digital Transformation* and *Others* 1.3 %	1.3 %	*Public Policy at the Local Level* 16.8 %
4	Europe	*Crisis Management and Resilience* and *Innovation and Digital Transformation* 2,7 %	2,7 %	*Governance Structures and Institutional Design* 16.2 %

[12] The research topics with the highest percentage indicated by respondents were: "Decentralisation and Multi-level Governance," "Governance Structures and Institutional Design," "Public Policy at the Local Level," "Local Democracy and Political Representation," "Public Management," "Urban, Regional and Rural Development," "Local Public Finance and Budgeting," "Comparative and International Perspectives," "Others." Only "Crisis Management and Resilience" ranked behind innovation and digital transformation as a research topic.

		Research area indicated by researchers		
	Geographical area	The research area LEAST interesting to researchers	Innovation and Digital Transformation (research percentage in a given geographical area)	The research area MOST interesting to researchers
5	Asia	*Crisis Management and Resilience* 3 %	6.4 %	*Decentralisation and Multi-level Governance* 17.4 %
6	Africa	*Innovation and Digital Transformation* 3.1 %	3.1 %	*Governance Structures and Institutional Design* 15.9 %

Source: own work based on Navarro & Cravacuore, 2025.

Research on local government does not always concern new technologies but is used in conducting such research or collecting large amounts of data, as in the case of research based on The Local Autonomy Index (LAI)[13]. In the second comprehensive version of the study ("LAI 2.0'), the measurements were refined and extended to countries on six continents(Ladner et al., 2025). The results of research based on data from Local Autonomy Index 2.0 (LAI 2.0) are interesting, in which the presentation includes the eleven variables, followed by the seven dimensions, and then finally the overall index (LAI). The research conclusions take into account differences depending on the fifty-seven countries' affiliations to the EU (European Union), CoE (Council of Europe) and OECD (Organisation for Economic Co-operation and Development)[14]. The main general trends show an increase in local

[13] The Local Autonomy Index (LAI) is a multi-dimensional conceptualisation and measurement of local autonomy initially developed in 2015. The first volume on the LAI was published in 2019, focusing on the construction of the index, its application to the European context to highlight various patterns of local autonomy and the study of its causes and consequences.

[14] The timespan covered goes from 1990 to 2020, except for the following ten countries where the time series starts at a later point (indicated in parentheses): Latvia (1991), Ukraine (1991), Albania (1992), Romania (1992), Andorra (1993), Malta (1993), South Africa (1994), Armenia (1996), Bosnia and Herzegovina (1996) and Kosovo (2000).

autonomy across all variables, dimensions and the index itself. Countries that have shown a recent decentralisation trend with overall decreasing scores for local autonomy (Hungary, Poland and Belarus), can also show stability or increases depending on which specific dimension is observed. On the other side, federalist countries show a different configuration of local autonomy when observing the dimensions, which opens the door to an interesting discussion on the link between local autonomy and regional authority in a multi-level governance context. However, what is important and indicative of the significant institutional role of the European Union in this regard is that degrees of local autonomy and their progressions vary depending on whether a country belongs to the EU, CoE or OECD. This raises questions about the impact of certain ratifications, one that is broadly developed in this volume being the European Charter of Local Self-Government (Navarro & Cravacuore, p. 56).

From a political scientist's point of view, research on the phenomenon of convergence[15] (Knopek, 1998, p. 139) in the implementation of new technologies by countries with similar cultural and historical resources (Vrabie & Krauze-Maślankowska, 2025) is interesting. They indicate that not only, as is the case in the EU, national and supranational digitisation policies are important in the context of implementing new technologies, but also the experiences of countries that have previously introduced similar solutions. The topic of implementing new technologies and digitisation models, as well as the AI policies of individual countries, deserves more detailed and in-depth research.

Research – central scope

Many studies are conducted at the supranational level (especially in the area of European Union regulations) or at the national level (Zhu et al., 2025). The results of studies from Asia, which is still considered a leader in the development of new technologies, seem to be of interest. As indicated not

[15] The concept of convergence is understood here as a term used in political transformation, referring to the adoption of certain characteristic features reflecting the conditions prevailing in Western countries (or countries at a "higher" level of economic and political development) by countries undergoing political transformation.

only by the IPSA research group, digitisation in this region also plays a role as a subject of research on local government in individual countries in the region (Liu et al., 2026). At the city level, British researchers examined how United Kingdom citizens perceive the use of AI in public sector decisions. In their research, they came to the conclusion that people prefer AI to have less decisional weight than various human decision-makers. People prefer AI to take up an advisory role, rather than a (co)decisive role. AI is seen as contributing more to output than to input and throughput legitimacy, and AI usage is seen as especially unsuited for decisions that are highly ideological (Haesevoets et al., 2024).

The exploratory work carried out by governments that attach importance to the digitisation of public administration not only at the central level should also be considered good practice. Poland conducted an exploratory study aimed at deepening knowledge about the state of implementation of new digital technologies in various types of local government units in Poland (W Drodze Ku Doskonałości Cyfrowej Raport Końcowy z Badania Rynku Na Temat Gotowości Wdrożenia, Poziomu Wiedzy i Wykorzystania Nowych Technologii Cyfrowych w Jednostkach Samorządu Terytorialnego, 2023). As the study shows[16], more than half of local government units plan to implement new digital technologies (but their use is no longer so obvious and expected).

In turn, the United States, with the help of researchers from the University of Pittsburgh, has designed a guide to be accessible as a "first step" for readers who have not yet considered adopting their governments' existing procurement processes for AI (E. Silva et al., 2025, p. 5).

Not all studies focus on the scale, quality and challenges of implementing new technologies at the local management and administration level. Some do the opposite – they look for reasons why digitalisation is almost absent from the local political agenda (like in the most likely case of Danish local governments, which constitutes a democratic problem because important priorities

---

[16] The survey covered 1,543 local government units in Poland. Units that reported no plans in this area pointed to a lack of funds to finance the process and no identified need for the technologies in question. The most common response among the local government units surveyed was the use of e-service-based solutions. Almost all of the surveyed units use them. The needs of citizens are the main reason for their introduction. Less often, they are implemented with a view to improving the internal operations of the office.

are then taken outside of the local political system). Existing quantitative research on setting policy agendas fail to explain why digitalisation is not on the local political agenda and four main barriers are identified blocking digitalisation from the local political agenda: Political role perception, lack of interest, lack of insight, and risks (Kristensen, 2023).

The research is not limited to the EU or the US; the topic is of interest to researchers on all continents (Paul Taire Okudolo & Ojakorotu, 2021; Syam et al., 2025).

Research – local and regional scope

There are many examples of research into the application of new technologies and the digitisation of public administration as a factor supporting the development of services at the local level, significantly more than those with a global research scope. However, when treated as case studies, they are extremely valuable, allowing not only model solutions to be identified, but also the imperfections of the solutions used and the risks associated with them to be "spotted" at the individual level. Local studies are being conducted, analysing, for example, the effectiveness of online services provided by local authorities (which recognise the existence of e-government encouraging the government to create good governance by meeting the community's needs for information and transparency) (Indar et al., 2024).

Many studies focus on challenges within a narrower scope, such as cybersecurity (Czuryk & Kostrubiec, 2019; Hoffman, 2024; Hoffman & Karpiuk, 2022; Kaczmarek, 2022) or ecology (Liu et al., 2026). When analysing the digital transformation of public services in Palu City (An Analytical Study on the Digitalization of Public Services through the "SanguPalu" Application), the ability to understand ICT hardware and software as well as digital operating systems has been effectively implemented. In the ethics dimension, the ability to adapt, think rationally, and prioritise ethical behaviour has also been appropriately applied. Regarding culture, the application has contributed to national awareness and identity in the digital realm. However, the safety aspect, particularly concerning personal data protection and digital security, has not been effectively implemented according to the research findings (Irfan & Haryono, 2025). A great deal of research concerns the field of health and management in the field of public health (Ahmad, 2025; Cross et al.,

2024; Faiyazuddin et al., 2025; Vu & Throne, 2024). The governance turn in political research has led to increased attention to informal institutions (IIGOs)[17] (Squatrito & Sommerer, 2025, p. 994). Do this "communities" use new technologies? Yes.

Conclusions

The aim of the bibliometric analysis was to examine the extent to which topics related to digital transformation (ICT, AI, digitisation) in the context of local government, local administration and local services are present in scientific literature, particularly from the perspective of challenges for the labour market and the organisation of employment in the public sector, which are part of the broader discourse on the "Future of Work." Six databases of various types were subjected to quantitative analysis: Scopus, Sage Journals, Google Scholar, Academia.edu, EBSCO, Springer, using three sets of search terms:

- ("new technologies" OR "AI" OR "digitalisation") AND "local government";
- ("new technologies" OR "AI" OR "digitalisation") AND "local administration";
- ("new technologies" OR "AI" OR "digitalisation") AND "local services."

The qualitative analysis revealed that most studies post-2020 examine the effectiveness of AI tools in urban governance, particularly in areas like transport, ecology, communication with residents, and predictive risk management. Yet, topics such as local political agenda-setting, implementation asymmetries, or interdisciplinary frameworks for ethical AI use remain peripheral. Surprisingly, digital exclusion (especially in terms of behavioural and socio-economic barriers)is rarely addressed in the context of public digitisation strategies, despite being a significant threat to equality and legitimacy in local governance. These findings highlight the fragmented nature of the literature and the need for a more integrated, citizen-oriented approach to studying AI in local public services. The results show that AI significantly

[17] For scholars of international relations this has contributed to recent scholarship that reveals a notable growth in the number of informal intergovernmental organisations (IIGOs).

improves city governance by optimising resource allocation, improving public service delivery, and enabling proactive problem-solving. For example, AI-based predictive analytics or communication tools (e.g. chatbots). It also identifies challenges such as data privacy, ethical concerns, and technology readiness, which are key for local governments(Smalec et al., 2025, p. 497).

It has been shown that research focuses on selected topics related to the use of new technologies (city management, primarily public transport and communication; monitoring threats; communication with citizens and increasing participation through applications and chatbots; supporting ecology). They can also be classified according to their scope. Surprisingly, the issue of digital exclusion of local community citizens is rarely mentioned in public policies related to digitisation and the use of new technologies. Although the European Union's digitalisation policies indicate specific digitalisation objectives, it should not be forgotten that digital exclusion is not only related to infrastructure (but also to behavioural limitations). In addition, exclusion can exist within a country between social groups (due to age and education) or between countries as a global digital divide between those with better and worse access to ICT (Posłajko, 2021, p. 38). In addition, together with changes in the job markets, twenty-first-century skills such as searching and evaluating information, solving problems, exchanging information or developing ideas in a digital context are perceived as essential. twenty-first-century skills are broader and more often on a conceptual level than digital skills (Van Laar et al., 2017).

Review studies are also being conducted. A separate issue that has not been addressed and certainly requires further research is the area of political communication, both during local election campaigns (where the use of new technologies is increasing due to limited funds and resources) and during the term of office of local executive and legislative bodies.

This preliminary study was intended to draw attention and provoke reflection. In this context and in relation to the issue of the "Future of work," there is a growing need to study new models of employment in local government (e.g. remote working, flexible working hours), the changing competences of civil servants (digital skills, AI literacy), and the impact of automation and digitisation on the organisational structure of local government. There is also a need for in-depth research into the impact of new technologies, digitisation and AI on the social legitimacy of public decisions, new forms of civic participation taking into account digital competences, digital exclusion in access to public administration, and differences between the implementation of solutions in the public and private sectors. Another interesting area for further research is the question of how the media shape discourses on the nature of the Internet (Wasilewski, 2020).

The results of this study provide a direct answer to the research question (RQ1) and hypothesis (H1). With regard to RQ1 (How is the issue of new technologies, including AI and digitalisation policies, researched in local government and local public services?), the bibliometric and qualitative analysis demonstrates that existing research is heavily concentrated on the strategic, governance-oriented and managerial dimensions of local government, particularly in areas such as smart city management, urban mobility, environmental monitoring, and digital communication with citizens. In contrast, significantly less scholarly attention is devoted to local administration as an executive structure and to local public services as sites of everyday interaction between citizens and public authorities, especially from the perspective of work organisation and employment. Concerning H1 (the incorporation of new technologies, including AI, improves the quality of local public services), the qualitative analysis provides partial confirmation of this hypothesis: the literature indicates that AI-based tools (e.g. predictive analytics, chatbots, data-driven decision-support systems) can enhance efficiency, responsiveness, and problem-solving capacity in local governance. However, these benefits are conditional and uneven, as the analysis also reveals persistent challenges related to data protection, ethical governance, organisational readiness, and cybersecurity, which may limit or even undermine service quality.

On the basis of these findings, four major research gaps can be identified:

- insufficient empirical research on the operational and labour-related consequences of digital transformation for local public administration;
- limited attention to changing employment models, skill requirements, and working conditions of local government employees in the context of the "Future of Work";
- a notable underrepresentation of digital exclusion as a policy and research problem, despite its relevance for equality and democratic legitimacy; and
- a lack of integrated studies addressing the impact of AI on the social legitimacy, accountability, and transparency of local public decision-making.

These gaps indicate that while the technological dimension of local digital transformation is relatively well explored, its social, organisational, and employment-related implications remain insufficiently theorised and empirically examined.

The results of this preliminary, non-complementary study also highlight certain research gaps, which would require further in-depth quantitative and qualitative research in order to draw specific conclusions. However, the study draws attention to the increasing number of studies in this area. The author also suggests increasing access to research results for local government representatives so that the implementation of new technologies is based on informed analysis and the role of technology as a means rather than an end in itself. This is particularly important in view of the phenomenon of digital exclusion, the atomisation of society and the increase in the participation of local communities.

Bibliography

A Definition of AI: Main Capabilities and Disciplines (2019). Definition Developed for the Purpose of the AI HLEG's Deliverables. European Commission.

Aditya, T., Ningrum, S., Nurasa, H., & Irawati, I. (2023). "Community Needs for the Digital Divide on the Smart City Policy". *Heliyon*, *9*(8), e18932. <https://doi.org/10.1016/j.heliyon.2023.e18932>.

Agbabiaka, O., Ojo, A., & Connolly, N. (2025). "Requirements for Trustworthy AI-Enabled Automated Decision-making in the Public Sector: A Systematic Review". *Technological Forecasting and Social Change*, 215, 124076. <https://doi.org/10.1016/j.techfore.2025.124076>.

Ahmad, M. (2025). "Regulating Intelligence: A Systematic Analysis of Safety, Ethics, and Equity in Artificial Intelligence Driven Healthcare". *Intelligence-Based Medicine*, 12, 100320. <https://doi.org/10.1016/j.ibmed.2025.100320>.

Akgunduz, D., & Mesutoglu, C. (2021). "STEM Education for Industry 4.0 in Technical and Vocational High Schools: Investigation of Teacher Professional Development". *Science Education International*, *32*(2), 172–181. <https://doi.org/10.33828/sei.v32.i2.11>.

Alizadeh, H., & Sharifi, A. (2023). "Toward a Societal Smart City: Clarifying the Social Justice Dimension of Smart Cities". *Sustainable Cities and Society*, *95*, 104612. <https://doi.org/10.1016/j.scs.2023.104612>.

Amankwah-Amoah, J. (2019). "Technological Revolution, Sustainability, and Development in Africa: Overview, Emerging Issues, and Challenges". *Sustainable Development, 27*(5), 910–922. <https://doi.org/10.1002/sd.1950>.

Arias, O., Fukuzawa, D., Le, D. T., & Mattoo, A. (2025). *Future Jobs: Robots, Artificial Intelligence, and Digital Platforms in East Asia and Pacific*. Washington, DC: World Bank. <https://doi.org/10.1596/978-1-4648-2199-8>.

Artificial Intelligence | Data-Smart City Solutions. (n.d.). Retrieved 5 January 2026, from <https://datasmart.hks.harvard.edu/artificial-intelligence>.

Batty, M., Axhausen, K. W., Giannotti, F., Pozdnoukhov, A., Bazzani, A., Wachowicz, M., Ouzounis, G., & Portugali, Y. (2012). "Smart Cities of the Future". *The European Physical Journal Special Topics, 214*(1), 481–518. <https://doi.org/10.1140/epjst/e2012-01703-3>.

Bharosa, N. (2022). "The Rise of GovTech: Trojan Horse or Blessing in Disguise? A Research Agenda". *Government Information Quarterly, 39*(3), 101692. <https://doi.org/10.1016/j.giq.2022.101692>.

Chumaceiro Hernández, A. C., Hernández G. De V., J. J., Pinto, L. B., Martínez, E. G., & Cardona Arce, Y. P. (2025). "More than Connectivity: Challenges of E-government in Countries with Special Situations". *Procedia Computer Science*, 272, 163–170. <https://doi.org/10.1016/j.procs.2025.10.192>.

Cropley, A. (2020). "Creativity-focused Technology Education in the Age of Industry 4.0". *Creativity Research Journal, 32*(2), 184–191. <https://doi.org/10.1080/10400419.2020.1751546>.

Cross, J. L., Choma, M. A., & Onofrey, J. A. (2024). "Bias in Medical AI: Implications for Clinical Decision-making". *PLOS Digital Health, 3*(11), e0000651. <https://doi.org/10.1371/journal.pdig.0000651>.

Czuryk, M., Janas, E., Karpiuk, M., Kostrubiec, J., & Szyjko, C. T. (Eds.). (2015). *Samorząd terytorialny w państwach Unii Europejskiej*. Akademia Obrony Narodowej.

Czuryk, M., & Kostrubiec, J. (2019). "The Legal Status of Local Self-government in the Field of Public Security". *Studia Nad Autorytaryzmem i Totalitaryzmem, 41*(1), 33–47. <https://doi.org/10.19195/2300-7249.41.1.3>.

De Fine Licht, K., & De Fine Licht, J. (2020). "Artificial Intelligence, Transparency, and Public Decision-making: Why Explanations are Key When Trying to Produce Perceived Legitimacy". *AI & Society, 35*(4), 917–926. <https://doi.org/10.1007/s00146-020-00960-w>.

de Fine Licht, K., & Folland, A. (2025). "AI in Public Decision-Making: A Philosophical and Practical Framework for Assessing and Weighing Harm and Benefit". *Public Administration*1–15. <https://doi.org/10.1111/padm.70029>.

Dolnicki, B. (Ed.). (2023). *Samorząd terytorialny jako forma upodmiotowienia społeczności lokalnych.* Wolters Kluwer Polska.

Dudzik, S. (2021). Podstawy prawne działania e-administracji a ochrona danych osobowych. In S. Dudzik, I. Kawka, & R. Śliwia (Eds.), *E-administracja: Skuteczna, odpowiedzialna i otwarta administracja publiczna w Unii Europejskiej* (pp. 13–28). Ksiegarnia Akademicka Publishing. <https://doi.org/10.12797/9788381386739.01>.

Emerging Technologies and the Future of Work in Europe | Digital Skills and Jobs Platform. (n.d.). Retrieved 2 December 2025, from <https://digital-skills-jobs.europa.eu/en/latest/news/emerging-technologies-and-future-work-europe>.

European Commission. (2022a). *Cyfrowa dekada Europy: Cele cyfrowe na 2030 r. „Drogą ku cyfrowej dekadzie."* Komisja Europejska. <https://www.consilium.europa.eu/pl/press/press-releases/2022/07/14/policy-programme-path-to-the-digital-decade-the-council-and-the-european-parliament-reach-a-provisional-agreement/>.

European Commission. (2022b). *Digital inclusion.* Komisja Europejska. <https://digital-strategy.ec.europa.eu/pl/node/9671>.

European Commission. Directorate General for Research and Innovation (2018). *Re-finding Industry: Defining Innovation.* Publications Office. <https://data.europa.eu/doi/10.2777/927953>.

European Commission. Directorate General for Research and Innovation (2021). *Industry 5.0: Towards a Sustainable, Human Centric and Resilient European Industry.* Publications Office. <https://data.europa.eu/doi/10.2777/308407>.

European Committee of the Regions. Commission for Economic Policy, Fondazione FORMIT, & Trilateral Research Limited. (2024). *AI and GenAI Adoption by Local and Regional Administrations.* Publications Office. <https://data.europa.eu/doi/10.2863/6007868>.

Faiyazuddin M, Rahman SJQ, Anand G, Siddiqui RK, Mehta R, Khatib MN, Gaidhane S, Zahiruddin QS, Hussain A, & Sah R. (2025). "The Impact of Artificial Intelligence on Healthcare: A Comprehensive Review of Advancements in Diagnostics, Treatment, and Operational Efficiency". *Health Science Reports, 8*(1), e70312. <https://doi.org/10.1002/hsr2.70312>.

Fischer-Abaigar, U., Kern, C., Barda, N., & Kreuter, F. (2024). "Bridging the Gap: Towards an Expanded Toolkit for AI-driven Decision-making in the Public Sector". *Government Information Quarterly, 41*(4), 101976. <https://doi.org/10.1016/j.giq.2024.101976>.

Goos, M., Manning, A., & Salomons, A. (2014). "Explaining Job Polarization: Routine-Biased Technological Change and Offshoring". *American Economic Review, 104*(8), 2509–2526. <https://doi.org/10.1257/aer.104.8.2509>.

Haesevoets, T., Verschuere, B., Van Severen, R., & Roets, A. (2024). "How Do Citizens Perceive the Use of Artificial Intelligence in Public Sector Decisions?". *Government Information Quarterly, 41*(1), 101906. <https://doi.org/10.1016/j.giq.2023.101906>.

Hoffman, I. (2024). "New Challenges of Local and Regional Public Service Provision: Platforms and Their Cybersecurity Issues". *Dot.Pl*, I, 79–88. <https://doi.org/10.60097/DOTPL/189319>.

Hoffman, I., & Karpiuk, M. (2022). "The Local Self-government's Place in the Cybersecurity Domain. Examples of Poland and Hungary". *Cybersecurity and Law, 7*(1), 171–190. <https://doi.org/10.35467/cal/151826>.

Indar, I. N., Razi, D. F., Atmansyah, L., Yani, A. A., & Ismail, N. (2024). "Digital Transformation of Public Services: An Analysis of the Effectiveness of Online Services at the Local Government Level". *Journal of Digital Sociohumanities, 1*(2), 92–101. <https://doi.org/10.25077/jds.1.2.92-101.2024>.

Ingwersen, P., & Serrano-López, A. E. (2018). "Smart city Research 1990–2016". *Scientometrics, 117*(2), 1205–1236. <https://doi.org/10.1007/s11192-018-2901-9>.

Irfan, M., & Haryono, D. (2025). "Digital Transformation in Public Service Delivery in Palu City: A Study on the Digitalization of Public Services Through the "SanguPalu" Application". *International Journal of Public Policy and Administration Research, 12*(4), 229–242. <https://doi.org/10.18488/74.v12i4.4568>.

Izdebski, H. (2020). *Samorząd terytorialny. Pionowy podział władzy*. Wolters Kluwer.

Kaczmarek, K. (2022). "Digital Competencies of the General Public and the State's Vulnerability to Cyberspace Threats". In *The Public Dimension of Cybersecurity* (pp. 29–37). Institute for Local Self-Government. <http://www.lex-localis.press/index.php/LexLocalisPress/catalog/book/ThePublicDimensionofCybersecurity>.

Kaiser, Z. R. M. A. (2024). “Smart Governance for Smart cities and Nations”. *Journal of Economy and Technology, 2*, 216–234. <https://doi.org/10.1016/j.ject.2024.07.003>.

Kapsa, I., & Musiał-Karg, M. (2020). “E-Government in Poland in Public Data and Opinions of Poles: Empirical Analysis”. In *Proceedings of the 13th International Conference on Theory and Practice of Electronic Governance*, pp. 419–429.

Knopek, J. (1998). *W Europie przemian konfliktów i kompromisów: Materiały pomocnicze dla studentów historii i politologii z zakresu transformacji ustrojowej*. Wydaw. Uczelniane WSP – Wyższej Szkoły Pedagogicznej.

Kolade, O., & Owoseni, A. (2022). “Employment 5.0: The Work of the Future and the Future of Work”. *Technology in Society*, 71, 102086. <https://doi.org/10.1016/j.techsoc.2022.102086>.

Kristensen, K. (2023). “Why Digitalization is NOT on the Local Political Agenda: Findings from Danish Local Governments”. *Scandinavian Journal of Public Administration*, 27(4), 52–68. <https://doi.org/10.58235/sjpa.2023.10663>.

Ladner, A., Keuffer, N., Bastianen, A., Baldersheim, H., Hlepas, N., Navarro, C., Steyvers, K., & Swianiewicz, P. (2025). *Dynamics and Issues of Local Autonomy: A Comparative Study*. Edward Elgar Publishing. <https://doi.org/10.4337/9781035337958>.

Lane, J.-E. (2002). *New Public Management* (1 edn). Routledge. <https://doi.org/10.4324/9780203467329>.

Liu, L., Xu, J., Zhang, Z., & Bi, Y. (2026). “Assessing the Digital Village Development in China and Its Driving Factors: An Analysis Using Online Media Data”. *Habitat International*, 168, 103707. <https://doi.org/10.1016/j.habitatint.2025.103707>.

Lubik-Reczek, N., Kapsa, I., & Musiał-Karg, M. (2020). *Elektroniczna partycypacja obywatelska w Polsce. Deklaracje i opinie Polaków na temat e-administracji i e-głosowania*. Wydawnictwo Naukowe Wydziału Nauk Politycznych i Dziennikarstwa.

Mahroof, K., Weerakkody, V., Hussain, Z., & Sivarajah, U. (2025). “Navigating Power Dynamics in the Public Sector through AI-driven Algorithmic Decision-making”. *Government Information Quarterly, 42*(3), 102053. <https://doi.org/10.1016/j.giq.2025.102053>.

Mark, D., & Morison, J. (2025). “Governing AI Decision-Making: Balancing Innovation and Accountability”. *Politics and Governance, 13*, 10245. <https://doi.org/10.17645/pag.10245>.

Mehdi, N., & Naz, T. (2025). "Governing the Intelligent Factory – Transforming Labor Law Through an Open-standards Framework for AI Governance in Industry 4.0". *Journal of Open Innovation: Technology, Market, and Complexity, 11*(4), 100690. <https://doi.org/10.1016/j.joitmc.2025.100690>.

Ministerstwo Cyfryzacji (2023). *W drodze ku doskonałości cyfrowej Raport końcowy z badania rynku na temat gotowości wdrożenia, poziomu wiedzy i wykorzystania nowych technologii cyfrowych w jednostkach samorządu terytorialnego*, p. 108. <https://www.gov.pl/web/ai/wdrazanie-technologii-w-samorzadach---raport-z-badania>.

Navarro, C., & Cravacuore, D. (2025). *Global Survey. Mapping Academic Research on Local Government and Politics (IPSA RC05 Comparative Studies on Local Government and Politics*, p. 19. International Political Science Association. <http://rc05.ipsa.org/public/Global_Survey_on_Local_Government_and_Politics_SEOULppt.pdf>.

Niesporek, A. (2025). "Global Civil Society and the Challenges of Global Democracy". *Journal of Modern Science, 64*(4), 121–144. <https://doi.org/10.13166/jms/214587>.

OECD. (2023). *Integrating Local Services for Individuals in Vulnerable Situations. OECD Local Economic and Employment Development (LEED) Papers*, 2023(08). <https://doi.org/10.1787/1596644b-en>.

Paul Taire Okudolo, I., & Ojakorotu, V. (2021). "Digitalization of Local Governance for Fostering Accelerated Attainment of the SDGs: Challenges and Prospects from a Nigerian Perspective". *African Journal of Development Studies (Formerly AFFRIKA Journal of Politics, Economics and Society)*, SI(1), 177–196. <https://doi.org/10.31920/2634-3649/2021/SIv1a9>.

Pietruch-Reizes, D. (2019). "Rola i znaczenie towarzystw naukowych w systemie nauki i kultury odradzającego się państwa polskiego". In *Rola towarzystw naukowych w rozwoju świadomości obywatelskiej i kulturowej*, pp. 45–56. Wydawnictwo Poznańskiego Towarzystwa Przyjaciół Nauk.

Podgórska-Rykała, J., & Pospieszna, P. (Eds.). (2024). *Innowacje deliberatywne: Inspiracje dla praktyków i teoretyków.* Fundacja Rozwoju Demokracji Lokalnej im. Jerzego Regulskiego: C. H. Beck.

Posłajko, R. (2014). "Rozwój europejskiej polityki cyfrowej". *Poliarchia, 2*(2), 37–61. <https://doi.org/10.12797/Poliarchia.02.2014.02.03>.

Rabe, W., M. Bondes, C. M. Abels, and G. Kostka. (2026). "Public Participation in China's State-Created ICT Spaces: Explaining

Participation Patterns." *Regulation & Governance* 20, no. 1: 64–89. https://doi.org/10.1111/rego.70090.

Regulation (EU) 2024/1689 of the European Parliament and of the Council of 13 June 2024 laying down harmonised rules on artificial intelligence and amending Regulations (EC) No 300/2008, (EU) No 167/2013, (EU) No 168/2013, (EU) 2018/858, (EU) 2018/1139 and (EU) 2019/2144 and Directives 2014/90/EU, (EU) 2016/797 and (EU) 2020/1828 (Artificial Intelligence Act) (Text with EEA relevance) PE/24/2024/REV/1. (n.d.). <https://eur-lex.europa.eu/legal-content/EN/TXT/?uri=CELEX%3A32024R1689>.

Reiter, R., & Klenk, T. (2019). "The Manifold Meanings of "Post-New Public Management" – A Systematic Literature Review". *International Review of Administrative Sciences, 85*(1), 11–27. <https://doi.org/10.1177/0020852318759736>.

Sætra, H. S. (2021). "A Typology of AI Applications in Politics". In A. Visvizi & M. Bodziany (Eds.), *Artificial Intelligence and Its Contexts* (pp. 27–43). Springer International Publishing. <https://doi.org/10.1007/978-3-030-88972-2_3>.

Silva, E., Johnson, N., Dotan, R., Eslami, M., Heidari, H., & Schwanke, B. (2025). "Procuring Public-Sector AI: Guidance for Local Governments". *SSRN Electronic Journal*. <https://doi.org/10.2139/ssrn.5227802>.

Silva, P., Tavares, A. F., Silva, T., & Lameiras, M. (2019). "The Good, the Bad and the Ugly: Three Faces of Social Media Usage by Local Governments". *Government Information Quarterly, 36*(3), 469–479. <https://doi.org/10.1016/j.giq.2019.05.006>.

Singh, S. K., & Sengupta, S. (2025). *Sovereign AI: Rethinking Autonomy in the Age of Global Interdependence* (Version 1). arXiv. <https://doi.org/10.48550/ARXIV.2511.15734>.

Smalec, A., Wanagos, M., Niemczyk, A., & Benková, E. (2025). *Artificial Intelligence (AI) in Local Governments: How Do Intelligent Technologies Improve City Management and Resident Communication?* In *Intelligent Management and Artificial Intelligence: Trends, Challenges, and Opportunities, Vol. 2: Proceedings of the 28th European Conference on Artificial Intelligence (ECAI 2025) – InMan Workshop* (pp. 497–510). Wydawnictwo Naukowe Uniwersytetu Szczecińskiego. <DOI: 10.18.276/978-83-8419-053-1-33>.

Squatrito, T., & Sommerer, T. (2025). "Informal Governance and Transnational Access in World Politics". *Regulation & Governance, 19*(4), 994–1014. <https://doi.org/10.1111/rego.12636>.

Syam, A., Sukri, & Hans, A. (2025). "E-Government and Digitalization as Catalysts for Organizational Transformation and Public Service Efficiency in Indonesian Local Governments". *KnE Social Sciences*, *10*(18), 1156–1164. <https://doi.org/10.18502/kss.v10i18.19542>.

Tjondronegoro, D. W. (2024). *Strategic AI Governance: Insights from Leading Nations* (Version 1). arXiv. <https://doi.org/10.48550/ARXIV.2410.01819>.

Tundys, B., Puzio, E., & Bachanek, K. (2022). *Smart city: Modele, generacje, pomiar i kierunki rozwoju. edu-Libri.*

Van Laar, E., Van Deursen, A. J. A. M., Van Dijk, J. A. G. M., & De Haan, J. (2017). "The Relation between 21st-century Skills and Digital Skills: A Systematic Literature Review". *Computers in Human Behavior*, 72, 577–588. <https://doi.org/10.1016/j.chb.2017.03.010>.

Vieira, M., Rua, O. L., & Arias-Oliva, M. (2023). "Impact of Open Innovation in Smart Cities: The Case Study of Köln (Germany)". *Journal of Open Innovation: Technology, Market, and Complexity*, 100068. <https://doi.org/10.1016/j.joitmc.2023.100068>.

Vrabie, C., & Krauze-Maślankowska, P. (2025). "Comparative Smart City Governance. Lessons from Poland for Advancing Romania's Urban Digital Transformation". *Transylvanian Review of Administrative Sciences* (Special Issue), 161–185. <https://doi.org/10.24193/tras.SI2025.9>.

Vu, T., & Throne, R. (2024). "Current Trends in AI Ethics for Software as a Medical Device (SaMD)". In R. Throne (Ed.), *Advances in Data Mining and Database Management*, pp. 145–164. IGI Global. <https://doi.org/10.4018/979-8-3693-3848-3.ch006>.

Wang, Z. (2025). "Generative AI-Making and State-Making: Sovereign AI Race and the Future of Digital Geopolitics". *Politics and Governance*, 13, 10222. <https://doi.org/10.17645/pag.10222>.

Wasilewski, K. (2020). "When Technology Meets Ideology". *First Monday*. <https://doi.org/10.5210/fm.v25i8.10817>.

Włodyka, E. (2021). "Why Do We Need E-government? Developing Basic Digital Skills of Administration Employees in Western Pomerania". *Acta Politica Polonica*, 52, 89–100. <https://doi.org/10.18276/ap.2021.52-08>.

Włodyka, E. M. (n.d.). Fundacja Rozwoju Demokracji Lokalnej, *Sztuczna inteligencja w administracji publicznej – doświadczenia i perspektywy*, IX.2023 r.

Yang, Y., & Khalid, N. A. (2025). "Smart Decision-Making in the Future City: A Social Innovation Perspective". *Journal of Cultural Analysis and Social Change*, *10*(2), 4654–4667. <https://doi.org/10.64753/jcasc.v10i2.2328>.

Zhu, J., Sinkkonen, E., & Mattlin, M. (2025). "Strategic Technology Competition Revisited: A National Innovation System Rationale for China's Artificial Intelligence Standardisation Strategy". *Telecommunications Policy*, *50*(2). <https://doi.org/10.1016/j.telpol.2025.103114>.

Digital storytelling as a space of learning creativity in HE

Marta Gliniecka[1]

ABSTRACT
Digital storytelling gained popularity in the 1990s in the United States. It is now used in many countries at various stages of education, from elementary school to higher education. It is an innovative teaching method that involves creating digital narratives combining images, video, music, and the voice of a narrator. Currently, the creation process can be further supported by artificial intelligence tools. Digital narratives can address various issues (cultural, social, political), thus deepening reflection on the surrounding world, shaping social skills, and developing social sensitivity.

The project will present the results of qualitative research conducted among pedagogy students representing two academic centres in Poland (the Pomeranian University in Słupsk and the Koszalin University of Technology). The study used triangulation of research methods (focus groups and visual research). The aim of the project was to determine what advantages students see in digital storytelling and what difficulties they encounter when creating digital narratives. It was also important to determine which digital tools – including AI – students use during the creation process and what elements (audiovisual, verbal) they include in their digital narratives.

Keywords: Digital storytelling, higher education, artificial intelligence

Introduction

The development of new media is changing our communication rituals. Digital devices such as computers, smartphones, and tablets shape our daily habits. Young people are connected to the internet around the clock, but they feel lonely (Turkle, 2011). Currently, an increasing number of AI tools are becoming available online, revolutionising the ways in which we gather information and acquire knowledge. Children, teenagers, and adults use digital devices not only for entertainment, but also for learning. They often watch videos on YouTube, listen to podcasts, comment on social media posts, and create their own multimedia content. According to Paul Levinson (2010), new media increase the democratisation of social life by offering opportunities for participation and engagement in culture. The multimedia

1 Koszalin University of Technology

has a potential for teaching and learning activity. Henry Giroux (2006, p. 183) describes this process:

> Citizens need to be multi-literate in ways that not only allow them access to new information and media-based technologies but also enable them to be border-crossers capable of engaging, learning from, understanding, and being tolerant of and responsible for matters of difference and otherness.

New media have created possibilities for sharing and collaborating with a wider audience – including an academic environment. Maria Cutajar (2019) points that using of technology, offers the opportunity to learn by participating in the co-creation of knowledge. It can help to develop learners' twenty-first century skills, such as digital literacy, problem-solving, collaboration, critical and creative thinking (Harrari, 2018).

It is becoming crucial for education to prepare young people to use new technologies, including generative AI, in a creative but also ethical way. Chiu and colleagues (2022) proposed three goals for AI education:

- preparing young people for life with AI,
- cultivating AI talents, and
- training future professionals across different fields to integrate AI in their jobs.

For instance, interesting qualitative research conducted in 2022 in secondary schools in Hong Kong, shows how teachers perceive AI education through their teaching experience. The researchers used a phenomenographic approach and identified six categories of teacher conceptions: technology bridging, interest stimulation, knowledge delivery, ethics establishment, capability cultivation, and intellectual development (Yau et al., 2023). It is important to teach young adults to use digital tools in a creative and reflective way. Digital tools should be used in education in the context of social and cultural issues:

> In the times of technological, political, social, and economic change it is easy to forget that the future of work is about people. Whatever problems will be solved – or created – by AI and other digital tools, they should be considered from the perspective of human well-being (Wasilewski, 2025, p. 9).

One of the tools for developing students' creativity and reflectiveness is digital storytelling. It is an innovative learning method based on creating short films that combine multimedia, including images, videos, music, and narration, which could be used to tell and reflect on unique experiences of human life and construct meaning. Digital storytelling combines traditional storytelling with new technologies. It offers the possibility to create one's own story about many topics, including culture diversity, nature, society, and human rights.

This method has gained popularity in America and many countries in Europe and can be used for various purposes for education. Digital storytelling was first introduced in the 1990s by Dana Atchley and Joe Lambert in San Francisco. They initiated a project called the "Center for Digital Storytelling" (Ramalia, 2023). Currently, this pedagogic tool has gained popularity among educators worldwide, particularly in higher education. It is important to learn about the perspective of students. I decided to check how students of pedagogy, perceive digital storytelling and AI tools in the context of developing creativity.

The benefits of digital storytelling in higher education

Through digital storytelling, students can enhance visual and media literacies. Moreover, they "may be encouraged to express their creativity, share their experiences, and reflect on their learning in a personalised and meaningful way" (Nik et al., 2024, p. 330). Many of research note that digital storytelling gives a voice to those who are marginalised (Clark & Adam, 2012; Robin, 2016). This method of conveying information through a narrative format, can be used for various purposes, such as teaching language skills, introducing cultures or even enhance prosocial behaviours.

Digital storytelling is a good way for developing social relationships and mutual trust (faith in someone's honesty and goodness). The belief that someone or something is trustworthy is the basis of effective educational activities. According to Elżbieta Perzycka and Maria Czerepaniak – Walczak (2014, s. 183) trust in education "can be seen as trust to the content of education, standards applicable in education, as well as trust to people – participants in educational interactions (...). Trust, as a personal disposition and social binder, is the purpose and medium of education."

Studies on digital storytelling have been conducted in many places across the United States, Europe, Asia or Australia. It has become a global field of study. For instance, the research from Australia, showed that DST could be as a tool to develop teacher-student relationship. Students aged 16 to 17 together with their teachers, participated in a digital storytelling workshop entitled "ASPIRing for our/your future." The workshop engaged young people from regional and remote areas in creating digital stories that reflected on their transition to higher education (O'Shea et al., 2019).

Digital storytelling is also an effective tool for visualising abstract learning topics to be more interesting. It can be used as learning material that involves students actively in deep learning. Alaa Sadik (2008) conducted research with students and teachers in Egypt. In this study, students were assigned to create digital stories using MS Photo Story software. After the students finished the digital stories project, they presented them in class. From the results of interviews, it can be shown that teachers believe that activities in the classroom by integrating technology in learning through digital narratives may improve students' comprehension of learning material. Students can be involved deeply in the process of creating digital narratives, either individually or collaboratively. "The use of DST in learning process does not only help learners in mastering learning material and technology skills but also increases learning motivation and practicing creative thinking skills" (Harjono & Wiryotinoyo, 2021, p. 262).

New media have opened new paths for enhancing creativity which is defined by the integration of critical thinking, imagination, flexibility, and the ability to generate novel solutions (Chen, 2024). Creating a short video allows young people to talk about their problems, interests and passions. Importantly, digital narratives allow students to create personal stories and present their own point of view. Daniel Ginting and colleagues (2024, p. 2) point that:

> Incorporating personalized principles into the narrative makes it even more engaging and relatable for the audience. Narrated videos have the advantage of using voice-over narration, which can evoke specific emotions; the storyteller can emotionally impact the viewers by carefully crafting the script and utilizing tone, pacing, and inflection. Connecting with emotions such as empathy, joy, sadness, or inspiration can make the content more memorable.

Creating digital narratives requires critical thinking. Students often utilise relevant images, videos, visual or sound effects to reinforce the message they want to convey to the audience. They can record a voice narration and look for the background music to make the story more engaging. Florin D.

Salajan and colleagues (2015) investigated the impact of narrated videos on adult students' motivation and engagement. The study found that storytelling effectively improved students' motivation and engagement.

Tenia Ramalia (2023, p. 7307) points that the process of creating digital storytelling involves several stages:

- planning, where students need to choose a story topic, identify the audience, and plan the story structure and create a story outline;
- production, where students gather materials such as relevant images, videos, background music, and use professional video editing software to edit them; and
- publication, where students share their stories with the audience.

Tenia Revalia (2023) found digital storytelling has significant benefits in higher education, such as improving students' critical thinking, planning, scriptwriting, the use of tools and software. In her opinion, this method can strengthen emotional connections with learning materials. The researcher identified several challenges that educators may face in the process of creating digital storytelling, such as the need for technical skills, limited access to devices and software. However, Tenia Revalia (2023, p. 7317) recommends integrating "digital storytelling into the curriculum, providing technical skill training for educators, providing resources and access to necessary devices and software, and supporting collaboration between educators and multimedia professionals."

Currently, there are many AI–powered digital tools, such as Photoshop, Canva or CupCut, that can enhance creativity of users. Generative AI can produce original content by learning from data and using complex algorithms to create human-like text, images, videos, music or voice narration. Nikolaos Pellas (2023) notes that educators can use generative AI platforms to create immersive experience and engaging stories that transcend traditional text-based narratives. "Through the fusion of technology and narrative, digital storytelling not only entertains but also educates, informs, and elicits emotions, thereby reshaping how stories are both created and consumed in the digital age" (Pellas, 2023, p. 1154). The study by Pellas results provide evidence that the use of generative AI platforms can significantly improve undergraduate students' narrative intelligence scores.

Some studies show that AI-facilitated digital storytelling could be an effective tool in higher education. For instance, the study by Yi-chen Chen (2024) aimed to investigate English as a Foreign Language (EFL) learners' perceptions and attitudes towards AI-facilitated digital storytelling. It was conducted at a private university in Taiwan in 2023. The research explored how Artificial Intelligence (AI) influences creative processes and how that creativity is perceived across different perspectives, including language learners, instructors and the audience. The findings indicated that generative AI could be a supportive tool and powerful facilitator in the creative process of EFL digital storytelling, but it does not replace the core creative input provided by humans.

There is a lot of interesting studies on this topic around the world. However, digital storytelling has not yet been applied extensively in polish education. That's the reason why I decided to conduct qualitative research on DST in higher education. This research aims to answer the following questions:

- What advantages do students see in digital storytelling?
- What challenges do students overcome in the process of making digital storytelling?
- What is the role of AI tool in digital storytelling videos?

Methodology

This project combines visual research with focus group interviews. The study involved twenty-five undergraduate students attending classes of pedagogy at two universities: University of Pomerania in Słupsk and Koszalin University of Technology. All participants were aged between 20 and 35 years old. They are pre-service pedagogues. Focus group interview is a qualitative technique for data collection. It consists of a small group of people and moderator who wants to explore participants' perceptions, feelings and ideas about a topic. According to Morgan (1997), focus groups may be used in three different ways:

- as Self-contained Method;
- as Supplementary Source of Data: They may be used to generate survey questionnaires, to develop a programme or intervention; or

- for Use in Multi-method Studies: They may be used effectively when several approaches such as in-depth interviews, participant observation are used to collect data.

This study employed triangulation and collected data from group interviews and digital narratives created by university students. To analyse the students' digital narratives, I used a compositional analysis developed by Gillian Rose (2010), which focuses on editing, colour, effects, and narration. Data from interviews and video documents was be coded and thematically analysed to identify patterns, themes, and emerging findings. I analysed data to identify the challenges and benefits of using digital storytelling in higher education.

At the beginning, in 2025, when I was teaching a class on information and communication technologies at Pomerania University in Słupsk, I asked my students (15 people) to create short digital narratives about their favourite books, movies, video games or TV series. They were allowed to use AI tools. Then, the students presented their work to the group and talked about their experiences and reflections related to filmmaking. The students created many interesting forms – from video reviews to movie trailers and videocasts. During the focus group interview, they talked about their feelings and difficulties.

At the same time, during the spring semester in 2025, I started class with pedagogy students in Koszalin University of Technology. Students took part in a competition to create a digital narrative on the concept of human social development. As a member of the jury, I watched all the digital narrated videos created by the students. Twenty films were created, which the students made in teams. The students created short films in various formats: stop-motion animations, multimedia presentations with music and voiceovers. As unlike the previous group, the students had not taken any classes related to the use of technology in education. They relied on their own experiences and skills. Finally, we selected four films, created by ten students, which were awarded for their original form (stop-motion animation, voice-over narration). I analysed the videos and conducted a group interview with the students. We talked about the programs they used. I was interested in how students used the AI tools to create digital stories.

Qualitative analysis of interview data and digital narratives

Based on the research conducted, the results show that students perceive DST as inspiring and challenging both. Some participants had some technical problems with using film editing software. They found it easier to use AI tools and create ready-made content.

The students use various programs to create digital stories, such as Canva, MyHeritage, HeyGen AI, and InVideo. Many participants created images with AI and added automatic subtitles to videos. Some students complained that AI tools are paid and require a subscription. It is worth noting that only three teams decided to create a film without using artificial intelligence tools. In two cases, they created interviews, like YouTubers. The students played roles using elements of drama. This approach demonstrated the creative use of technology in education. Data from two focus group interviews show how students perceive DST-based AI:

- "It was a difficult task, but I found the process of creating digital narratives exciting. I enjoy editing clips and adding soundtracks. DST is a powerful educational tool, so I intend to use it in my future work with children."
- "Generative AI allows me to generate many images and sound effects. I don't like recording my voice, so I used free AI tools that I learned about in class to create a voice-over."
- "I didn't use any AI tools. I found many photos on the website and recorded the voice-over myself."
- "I used AI tools to create visual segments – photos and videos, but I didn't mention this in my film."
- "Thanks to artificial intelligence, I was able to turn old photographs of famous people into stunning, animated videos. It was an incredible adventure."
- "I faced technical challenges in video editing. AI tools are very useful, but expensive."
- "I encountered challenges in organising the story flow and finding relevant materials. I overcame these challenges by teamwork."

Although the students faced technical challenges, they discovered new talents and passions. Two people said that after this task, they felt they could create their own video blog about literature. During the film presentation, the students felt appreciated by the audience, who showed their enthusiasm and rewarded them with applause. They paid attention to feedback from friends and instructor.

I found that creating digital narratives increases engagement and allows students to show their personal perspective. For example, one woman created a video review of a book showing the problems of children on the autism spectrum. It was important to her because her seven-year-old son also struggles with this problem. The boy appeared in the video with his mother.

The students also created many interesting videos with avatars and used stop-motion animation. Some students used a technology to create realistic video footage with famous deceased people, such as Sigmund Freud or Eric H. Erikson. In their digital narratives, they used both material found on social media (TikTok, Instagram) and material generated by AI. Unfortunately, they paid no attention to copyright or licensing issues. In contrast, participants in IT classes made better use of AI functions in digital narratives. This made me realise how important it is to talk to students about the ethical aspects of using AI in digital projects. The table below shows which AI elements students used in their digital stories and what kind of applications they know.

Table 1: The use of AI by students from two universities to create digital storytelling

Type of digital story	Digital tools	AI functions	Number of students
Trailer	Imovie CupCut	Automatic subtitle generation	6 (24 %)
Video review of book, film or game	CupCut Canva Chat GPT 4.o PXLR AI	Generating images in the form of photographs and illustrations and videos	12 (48 %)
Podcast and videocast	InVideo AI RunWay AI HeyGen AI IlElevenLabs	Creating avatars Elements of stop-motion animation Creating a voice-over	5 (20 %) 3 (12 %) 3 (12 %)
Interview with real of fictional person	Movavi MyHeritage Deep Nostalgia	Using animated photos of deceased people	5 (20 %)
Multimedia presentation	Canva, PowerPoint Prezi AI	Magic eraser, image editing with AI, animation effects	20 (80 %)

It is worth noting that only 50 % of the research participants used AI to generate visual materials. This may be related to the fact that most applications are so expensive, and students cannot afford the premium versions of the programs. Only a few students used digital tools to create automatic subtitles for a film (24 %) or to produce a voice-over (12 %). At the same time, many people create traditional presentations in programs such as Canva, which also offers users a free version.

It should be emphasised that we have access to many free online tools, including those for creating voiceovers in podcasts. However, only a few of participants used this option, which suggests that students don't always have sufficient digital skills. I noticed that participants who discussed AI tools during classes used them in a more deliberate way.

Conclusions

For many years, I have been interested in the educational potential of storytelling. People create stories in various forms to share their experiences and feelings. In the age of new media, students can create our own visual messages, such as blogs, podcasts, photos and films (Gliniecka, 2020). Creating digital stories helps develop positive traits such as creativity, intelligence and empathy. It helps us to understand others better. For example, when we create a podcast about the challenges faced by refugees, we can imagine what we would do if we were in their place. Creating digital narratives opens our eyes to different perspectives. These stories make us reflect on important values such as responsibility, solidarity, tolerance and community. Therefore, I believe that digital storytelling is a space for creative teacher training. This is a great way for teachers to engage their students. Through digital stories, they can express their opinions and discover new talents.

The study highlights the importance of creating digital narratives reflectively. It can be observed that students who create digital stories, develop various skills. They:

- learn to express complex ideas clearly
- gain confidence and a deeper ability to connect with an audience
- develop essential skills like critical thinking, creativity and collaboration

- enhance narrative skills
- build a conviction that their voices truly matter.

Additionally, students learn how to use technology, including AI tools and develop their digital skills, like using professional software for video and audio editing. However, this study show that undergraduate students use many AI tools and platforms to create digital narratives, but not always ethically. The finding indicates that adult students who had previously learned about generative artificial intelligence used these tools as support, for example, to record a voice-over or generate images. On the other hand, students who did not have such classes, created ready-made films with AI, without ethical dilemmas. It's interesting that only several people created digital narrated videos themselves without AI tools.

I think, students still need time to learn the ropes of using AI in education. The academic teachers should help them to use new technologies in their educational projects. Fatin N. Tarigan and colleagues (2024, p. 2) point that DST-based AI has a positive impact on the educational process:

> By engaging with these technologies, students learn to create meaningful narratives and become adept at navigating and leveraging digital tools for communication, collaboration, and problem-solving. Consequently, these skills prepare them for upcoming learning endeavours and professional opportunities in an interconnected digital world.

A key aspect of this issue is striking the balance between the use of AI tools and one's own creativity. From a pedagogical perspective, it is worth nothing that technology can be a source of inspiration, but it should not replace humans in the creative process. In antiquity Plutarch stated that "the mind is not a vessel to be filled, but a fire to be kindled."

To summarise, these findings have important implications for educators. The results suggest that students perceived digital storytelling as an effective tool for the conveying of information. The study contributes to understanding how we can introduce this method into the higher education curriculum. It should be noted that this study was limited to several cases. Due to the qualitative nature of the research, the findings cannot be generalised to all contexts. Future research could explore how academic teachers use digital tools in educational process.

Bibliography

Chen, Y.- chen. (2024). "Perceptions of AI-facilitated Creativity in Language Education: A Study on Digital Storytelling". *The JALT CALL Journal*, 20(3), 2089, 1–27. <https://doi.org/10.29140/jaltcall.v20n3.2089>.

Chiu, T. K. F., Meng, H., Chai, C. S., King, I., Wong, S., & Yeung, Y. (2022). "Creation and Evaluation of a Pre-tertiary Artificial Intelligence (AI) Curriculum". *IEEE Transactions on Education*, 65(1), 30–39. <https://doi.org/10.1109/TE.2021.3085878>.

Clarke, R., & Adam, A. (2012). "Digital Storytelling in Australia: Academic Perspectives and Reflections". *Arts and Humanities in Higher Education*, 11(1–2), 157–176. <https://doi.org/10.1177/1474022210374223>.

Cutajar, M. (2019). "Teaching Using Digital Technologies: Transmission or Participation?" *Education Sciences*, 9(3), 226. <https://doi.org/10.3390/educsci9030226>.

Czerepaniak-Walczak, M., & Perzycka, E. (2014). "Trust in Educational Interactions in Higher Education Institutions: Examination as an Experience of Trust". *The New Educational Review*, 36, 182–193. <https://cejsh.icm.edu.pl/cejsh/element/bwmeta1.element.ojs-doi-10_15804_tner_14_36_2_14>.

Ginting, D., Woods, R. M., Barella, Y., Limanta, L. S., Madkur, A., & How, H. E. (2024). "The Effects of Digital Storytelling on the Retention and Transferability of Student Knowledge". *Sage Open*, 14(3), 1–17. <https://doi.org/10.1177/21582440241271267>.

Giroux, H. A., & Robbins, C. G. (2006). *The Giroux Reader*. New York, NY: Routledge.

Gliniecka, M. (2020). *Multimedialne opowieści w blogach nastolatków. Od sieciowego ekshibicjonizmu ku autoekspresji [Multimedia stories in teenagers' blogs. From online exhibitionism to self-expression]*. Słupsk: Wydawnictwo Akademii Pomorskiej.

Harjono, H., & Wiryotinoyo, M. (2021). "Exploring the Benefits of Digital Storytelling for Enhancing Teaching and Learning". *Advances in Engineering Research*, 205, 262–265. <https://doi.org/10.2991/aer.k.210825.047>.

Harari, Y. N. (2018). *21 Lessons for the 21st Century*. Random House.

Levinson, P. (2012). *New New Media: International Edition*. London: Pearson.

Morgan, D. L. (1997). *Focus Groups as Qualitative Research*. Newbury Park: Sage.

Nik, E., Gauci, R., Ross, B., & Tedeschi, J. (2024). "Exploring the Potential of Digital Storytelling in a Widening Participation Context". *Educational Research*, 66(3), 329–346. <https://doi.org/10.1080/00131881.2024.2362336>.

O'Shea, S., Southgate, E., Jardine, A., & Delahunty, J. (2019). "Learning to Leave or "Striving to Stay": Considering the Desires and Decisions of Rural Young People in Relation to Post-Schooling Futures". *Emotion, Space and Society*, 32, 100587. <https://doi.org/10.1016/j.emospa.2019.100587>.

Ramalia, T. (2023). "Digital Storytelling in Higher Education: Highlighting the Making Process". *Journal on Education*, 6, 7307–7319. <https://doi.org/10.31004/joe.v6i1.3993>.

Robin, B. R. (2016). "The Power of Digital Storytelling to Support Teaching and Learning". *Digital Education Review*, 30, 17–29. <https://doi.org/10.1344/der.2016.30.17-29>.

Rose, G. (2001). *Visual Methodologies: An Introduction to the Interpretation of Visual Materials*. London: Sage.

Salajan, F. D., Schreiber, J. B., & Harteis, C. (2015). "The Impact of Storytelling on Adult Learners' Motivation and Engagement". *International Journal of Continuing Engineering Education and Life-Long Learning*, 25(3), 306–321.

Sadik, A. (2008). "Digital Storytelling: A Meaningful Technology-Integrated Approach for Engaged Student Learning". *Education Tech Research Development*, 56, 487–506. <https://doi.org/10.1007/s11423-008-9091-8>.

Tarigan, F. N., Hasibuan, S. A., & Nurmayana. (2024). "Application and Challenges of Digital Storytelling Based Artificial Intelligence for Language Skills: A Narrative Review". *SALTeL Journal (Southeast Asia Language Teaching and Learning)*, 7(1), 1–8. <https://doi.org/10.35307/saltel.v7i1.117>.

Turkle, S. (2011). *Alone Together: Why We Expect More from Technology and Less from Each Other*. Basic Books.

Wasilewski, K. (2025). "Introduction". In K. Wasilewski (Ed.), *Digital Humanities and Digital Skills in the Future of Work*, pp. 7–17. Berlin: Peter Lang.

Yau, K.W., CHAI, C.S., Chiu, T.K. et al. (2023). "A Phenomenographic Approach on Teacher Conceptions of Teaching Artificial Intelligence (AI) in K-12 Schools". *Education and Information Technologies*, 28, 1041–1064. <https://doi.org/10.1007/s10639-022-11161-x>.

Human rights in the age of digital surveillance: Challenges for the Strasbourg standard – selected issues

Maria Ochwat[1]

ABSTRACT
This article analyses the challenges that digital surveillance poses to the protection of human rights under the European Convention on Human Rights. Traditional protection mechanisms, including the proportionality test and the definition of a "victim," do not fully address the mass, systemic, and transnational nature of contemporary surveillance practices. An analysis of the case law of the European Court of Human Rights (ECtHR) shows that chilling effects and indirect restrictions on freedom of expression remain insufficiently considered within the Strasbourg standard. The final section proposes recommendations for the Council of Europe and other actors, including strengthening ex ante mechanisms, expanding the definition of "victim," adapting the proportionality test, taking chilling effects into account, adjusting jurisdictional frameworks to transnational surveillance, and educating citizens on digital rights. Implementing these recommendations could enhance the effectiveness of protecting individual rights in the era of digital surveillance.

Keywords: Human rights, digital surveillance, human rights challenges in the era of digital surveillance, European Court of Human Rights and digital surveillance

Introduction

Digital surveillance, understood as the collection and analysis of personal data using new technologies, has become a key element of contemporary security and information management (Lyon, 2018; Zuboff, 2019). It encompasses both state and private sector activities, including monitoring communications, collecting metadata, and using artificial intelligence to predict human behaviour. Such practices undoubtedly infringe human rights, particularly the right to privacy and freedom of expression (De Hert & Papakonstantinou, 2018). Unfortunately, traditional human rights protection mechanisms do not always keep pace with technological developments, so contemporary surveillance often requires reinterpretation of existing legal categories to effectively protect individuals (Kuner, 2020a).

[1] The John Paul II Catholic University of Lublin

The purpose of this article is to examine whether current standards for protecting privacy and freedom of expression under the ECtHR genuinely safeguard individuals in the age of digital surveillance, while also providing a list of recommendations whose implementation could significantly strengthen human rights protection in this area. The article includes an analysis of ECtHR case law and a review of scholarly literature to assess the effectiveness of human rights protection in the digital surveillance era and to identify recommendations for the Council of Europe and other international actors.

Digital surveillance as a challenge to human rights

To understand digital surveillance and its impact on human rights, it is necessary to examine its forms, types of data collected, the role of artificial intelligence and big data, and the chilling effect. Digital surveillance takes various forms that complicate traditional understandings of interference with individual rights.

Mass surveillance involves the systematic collection of data from large groups of people, regardless of suspicion of wrongdoing, creating significant risks to privacy (Lyon, 2018). Examples include state programs that intercept and analyse billions of electronic messages and metadata from citizens' daily activities. Targeted surveillance focuses on selected individuals or groups based on specific criteria, enabling precise interventions, although it still carries the risk of excessive intrusion into private life (Kuner, 2020b). The type of data under surveillance is particularly significant for human rights. Traditionally, this concerned the content of communications, such as letters or telephone calls. In the digital era, the importance of metadata – information about the time, location, frequency, and recipients of communications – has increased. Although metadata does not reveal the content of conversations, its analysis allows for the creation of detailed profiles of individuals' behaviours and social networks, potentially limiting their autonomy and privacy (De Hert & Papakonstantinou, 2018; Zuboff, 2019).

Furthermore, AI algorithms and big data systems, including predictive policing, enable the prediction of citizens' behaviours and risk assessment, raising questions about algorithmic discrimination and the proportionality of interference with human rights (Kuner, 2020c). The chilling effect refers to the phenomenon whereby awareness of potential surveillance leads individuals to self-censor and limit participation in public debate, threatening the exercise of freedom of expression (Penney, 2016).

All these elements indicate that traditional understandings of interference with private life (Article 8) and freedom of expression (Article 10) under the European Convention on Human Rights require reinterpretation in the context of digital surveillance. Mass and targeted surveillance, metadata analysis, AI use, and the chilling effect introduce new threats to individuals that do not fit within existing privacy and free expression frameworks, posing a serious challenge to ECtHR jurisprudence.

The right to respect for private life and freedom of expression in the age of digital surveillance

Digital surveillance undoubtedly has a significant impact on human rights, in particular the right to privacy (Article 8) and freedom of expression (Article 10) under the European Convention on Human Rights. To better understand the case law of the European Court of Human Rights (ECtHR) in Strasbourg regarding digital surveillance, it is useful to briefly clarify the essence of the right to privacy and freedom of expression.

The right to privacy is guaranteed by the Universal Declaration of Human Rights (1948, Article 12), the International Covenant on Civil and Political Rights (1966, Article 17), Article 8 of the European Convention on Human Rights, and Article 7 of the Charter of Fundamental Rights of the European Union (2000). According to Article 8(1) ECHR, "Everyone has the right to respect for his private and family life, his home, and his correspondence." The concept of private life is broad and difficult to define precisely. Based on ECtHR case law, it encompasses not only the right to live according to one's own wishes without external control but also the right to establish and maintain relationships with others in order to develop and realise one's personality (Botta v. Italy, 1998). It includes, inter alia, the right to "personal development" (Bensaid v. United Kingdom, 2001) and individual autonomy (Pretty v. United Kingdom, 2002). The significance of this provision and its protection extend beyond the private sphere of family relations and take on a social dimension (Armonas v. Lithuania, 2008).

Furthermore, the Court has held that the concept of private life covers aspects such as gender identity, sexual orientation, and sexual life; the right to respect for decisions regarding childbearing (S.H. and Others v. Austria, 2011); the right to a name and elements related to image rights (S. and Marper v. United Kingdom, 2008); and personal information that individuals can reasonably expect not to be published without their consent (Flinkkilä and Others v. Finland, 2010), including medical data regarding health and treatment (Avilkina and Others v. Russia, 2013). Ethnic identity is also a crucial aspect of private life. In Aksu v. Turkey (2012), the Court recognised that any negative stereotype about a group, if sufficiently entrenched, can affect members' sense of identity, self-worth, and confidence, thereby impacting the private life of each member.

It is important to note that such a broad construction of Article 8 ECHR does not imply protection of every activity in which a person engages jointly with others. It does not cover relationships so wide and indeterminate that it is difficult to see a direct link between state action or inaction and an individual's private life (Gough v. United Kingdom, 1980). Similarly, the fact that an activity is prohibited under criminal law does not preclude its protection under the right to privacy (A.D.T v. United Kingdom, 2000). In certain circumstances, Article 8 also encompasses the right to respect for reputation, business premises, and offices where activities are conducted. The Court has also recognised that professional activity and business operations fall within the notion of private life (Niemietz v. Germany, 1992). Sexual life, including sexual orientation, constitutes the most intimate sphere of private life (Dudgeon v. United Kingdom, 1985) and is protected under Article 8; however, the right to privacy does not cover sexual activities conducted professionally for remuneration.

Article 8 further guarantees, under certain conditions, the right to reputation (Niemietz v. Germany, 1992) and protection against potential attacks on reputation (Karakó v. Hungary, 2009) as well as honour (Sanchez Cardenas v. Norway, 2007). Protection under Article 8 extends to criticism in public debate, including matters of honour and reputation (Pfeifer v. Austria, 2007). To qualify, an attack must reach a certain level of gravity and cause harm to the individual's enjoyment of the right to privacy (A. v. Norway, 2009). However, Article 8 does not cover predictable loss of reputation resulting from one's own actions, such as committing a crime (Sidabras and Džiautas v. Lithuania, 2004).

The Court has held that a person's image is a core attribute of personality, enabling distinction from others and requiring control over its public use. This includes the right to refuse consent for publication, photographing, storing, and copying images by others (Reklos and Davourlis v. Greece, 2009), including video recordings (De La Flor Cabrera v. Spain, 2014). Even an entry in a police database may harm a person's reputation and hinder daily life, particularly if information can be transmitted to other authorities (Khelili v. Switzerland, 2011; Mikolajová v. Slovakia, 2011), which is highly relevant in the context of automated data processing today.

In Hilton v. United Kingdom (1988), the Commission held that anyone demonstrating a reasonable likelihood of systematic data collection and storage by authorities may claim victim status under Article 8 ECHR, even if the data were collected in public spaces or concern professional or public activities.

The Court has also examined cases involving GPS surveillance, such as tracking an individual's car, and storing location data in public spaces. It recognised that such surveillance differs from other visual or acoustic monitoring as it reveals more information about behaviour, opinions, and feelings (Uzun v. Germany, 2010). In Rotaru v. Romania, the Court held that systematic collection and storage of personal information by the state, even without active monitoring, falls within the scope of private life (Rotaru v. Romania, 2000). Examples of such interference include phone tapping, mail interception (Klass and Others v. Germany, 1978), identity verification interrogations (Friedl v. Austria, 1994), and other state actions requiring supervision in line with democratic requirements (Lupsa v. Romania, 2006).

The ECtHR consistently recognises that Article 8 ECHR covers modern forms of digital surveillance, including mass interception of electronic communications. Even the mere possibility of secret surveillance constitutes an interference with the right to privacy, regardless of whether communications are actually examined (Klass and Others v. Germany, 1978). The Court has established standards for assessing surveillance compliance with Article 8, emphasising the importance of legal quality, precise specification of scope, objectives, and mechanisms limiting state discretion (Weber and Saravia v. Germany, 2006; Zakharov v. Russia, 2015). In Big Brother Watch and Others

v. United Kingdom (2021), the Court held that bulk data collection is not automatically incompatible with the Convention but requires comprehensive safeguards covering the entire data processing chain and independent judicial or quasi-judicial review. Overall, ECtHR case law demonstrates that the right to privacy remains a cornerstone of a democratic state under the rule of law, and surveillance measures must be based on predictable law, minimise interference, and ensure effective independent oversight (Big Brother Watch and Others v. United Kingdom, 2021; Zakharov v. Russia, 2015).

Freedom of expression is guaranteed by Article 10 ECHR, as well as other instruments such as Article 19 of the Universal Declaration of Human Rights, Articles 19 and 20 of the International Covenant on Civil and Political Rights, and Articles 12 and 13 of the Convention on the Rights of the Child. A central concept for freedom of expression is that of "expression." The Human Rights Committee elaborated on its essential interpretation in G. McIntyre and Others v. Canada (1993), stating that expression encompasses ideas and opinions, messages, or information of any content – political, cultural, artistic, commercial (as advertising) – unless prohibited under Article 20 of the ICCPR (i.e. war propaganda or advocacy of national, racial, or religious hatred constituting incitement to discrimination, hostility, or violence). Expression may be articulated in any manner chosen by the author, including print, writing, orally, or as a work of art; each form should be treated equally, without differentiating protection based on format (Ballantyne, Davidson & McIntyre v. Canada, Communication Nos. 359/1989 & 385/1989, 1993).

The ECtHR has repeatedly addressed the limits of freedom of expression. In Handyside v. United Kingdom, it held that "freedom of expression is one of the essential foundations of a democratic society, a basic condition for its progress and for the self-fulfillment of every individual" (Handyside v. United Kingdom, 5493/72, 1976). This freedom may encompass behaviour that, if assessed without context or motive, could appear to disrupt public order. The Court has emphasised enabling citizens to freely participate in discussions of matters of public concern (Sürek v. Turkey, 26682/95, 1999). Protection under Article 10 extends to all types of expression, conveying opinions, ideas, or information, regardless of content or means, particularly political speech (Nilsen & Johnsen v. Norway, 23118/93, 1999), matters of public interest, and artistic expression (Müller & Others v. Switzerland, 25/1986/123/174, 1988).

Public debate in such matters can often be harsh, even vulgar. Participants may use exaggeration and provocation (Haguenauer v. France, 34050/05, 2010) and are entitled to some degree of intemperance (Prager & Oberschlick v. Austria, 15974/90, 1995). In issues of public significance, such as health, open debate must also allow small or informal groups to participate, as they act as public watchdogs, similar to the media, and their activity deserves equivalent protection (Youth Initiative for Human Rights v. Serbia, 48135/06, 2013). Conducting such public oversight is not only a right but an obligation (Lingens v. Austria, 9815/82, 1986).

Criticism is also protected. Acceptable limits of criticism are broader toward politicians and their public actions than private individuals. Politicians, by virtue of their role, must tolerate even particularly harsh attacks (Couderc Hachette Filipacchi Associés v. France, 40454/07, 2012).

The presentation of a specific subject may, depending on circumstances such as time and place, be neutral or constitute expression protected under Article 10 (Fáber v. Hungary, 40721/08, 2012). The same applies to symbolic expression, where context determines protection (Öllinger v. Austria, 76900/01, 2006; Vajnai v. Hungary, 33629/06, 2008). Protected expression also includes concrete behaviours, e.g. public nudity (Gough v. United Kingdom, 49327/11, 2014), cutting a ribbon from a wreath laid by the president (Shvydka v. Ukraine, 17888/12, 2014), or displaying banners while burning flags and portraits of the president (Christian Democratic People's Party v. Moldova, 25196/04, 2009).

Freedom of expression is exercised in part through the media, which the ECtHR has paid particular attention to. The Court holds that

> freedom of expression is one of the essential foundations of a democratic society, a basic condition for its progress and for the self-fulfillment of every individual. It applies not only to information or ideas received favorably or regarded as harmless or indifferent but also to those that offend, shock, or disturb the State or any sector of the population. Such are the requirements of pluralism, tolerance, and broadmindedness, without which there is no democratic society (Handyside v. United Kingdom, 5493/72, 1976).

The Court further emphasises that the press, while bound by certain limits, has the right to disseminate reliable information and ideas on all matters of public concern (The Sunday Times v. United Kingdom, 6538/74, 1979). Serious journalism cannot exist without confidential sources (Telegraaf Media

Nederland Landelijke Media B.V. & Others v. Netherlands, 34085/96, 2001). Arbitrary hindrance of journalists by authorities may amount to censorship (Dammann v. Switzerland, 77544/01, 2006).

The Internet differs from traditional media in the scope of information collection and dissemination, necessitating specific regulation (Editorial Board of Pravoye Delo & Shtekel v. Ukraine, 33044/05, 2011). States must provide legal frameworks allowing journalists to access online information without risk of sanctions (Editorial Board of Pravoye Delo & Shtekel v. Ukraine, 33044/05, 2011).

Applying surveillance measures to journalists constitutes a serious interference with freedom of expression and requires rigorous justification (Telegraaf Media Nederland Landelijke Media B.V. & Others v. Netherlands, 34085/96, 2001). Bulk interception of communications may discourage journalists from contacting confidential sources and informants from disclosing information in the public interest (Big Brother Watch & Others v. United Kingdom, 58170/13, 2021).

Whistleblowers revealing information on public sector wrongdoing in the public interest receive special protection (Guja v. Moldova, 14277/04, 2008). Surveillance-related interference must be subject to strengthened procedural safeguards, including independent, preferably judicial, oversight (Big Brother Watch & Others v. United Kingdom, 58170/13, 2021; Telegraaf Media Nederland Landelijke Media B.V. & Others v. Netherlands, 34085/96, 2001).

Overall, ECtHR case law indicates that in the era of digital surveillance, freedom of expression and press freedom are particularly vulnerable to indirect restrictions, which do not always take the form of direct censorship. Surveillance measures interfering with communication must meet the highest standards of legality, necessity, and proportionality, and, in the case of journalists and whistleblowers, be subject to especially rigorous oversight (Big Brother Watch & Others v. United Kingdom, 58170/13, 2021; Goodwin v. United Kingdom, 17488/90, 1996; Guja v. Moldova, 14277/04, 2008).

Limitations of the European Convention on Human Rights in the context of digital surveillance

Digital surveillance reveals certain limitations of the human rights protection standard based on the European Convention on Human Rights (ECHR).

These limitations do not result from a lack of protection provided by the European Court of Human Rights (ECtHR), but from the fact that the Convention was adopted in a different context, in which interferences with individual rights were more visible and could be individually identified. In this context, particular attention should be paid to issues such as the reactive nature of Strasbourg protection, the understanding of the concept of "victim," the effectiveness of the proportionality test, the problem of chilling effects and indirect violations of rights, as well as the transnational character of surveillance and the resulting jurisdictional difficulties.

The reactive nature of the Strasbourg standard indicates that it poorly addresses the preventive and continuous dimension of modern forms of surveillance. The ECHR protection system is fundamentally based on ex post review. This means that the interference must already have occurred to be assessed by the Court. Digital surveillance, however, operates continuously, often invisible to the individual, and is based on the logic of preventing potential threats. As noted by the UN Special Rapporteur on freedom of expression, post hoc protection cannot effectively counter mass surveillance, which is based on "data collection in advance" (Kaye, 2019). In these circumstances, ex ante safeguards – including clear legal bases, independent oversight, and limitations on the scope of surveillance at the design stage – become crucial. Nevertheless, the Strasbourg standard still primarily focuses on evaluating the legality of interference after the fact. Douwe Korff further criticises this approach, noting that the ECtHR applies a fundamentally reactive method in surveillance cases, which is inadequate for addressing systemic and structural threats to individual rights (Korff, 2012). Importantly, the Council of Europe itself recognises that surveillance – especially mass surveillance – requires particularly strict safeguards, since the mere possibility of unlimited data collection may constitute an interference with private life (Council of Europe, 2023). Post hoc protection is therefore insufficient to fully mitigate the effects of surveillance, which are often permanent and irreversible.

Digital surveillance also challenges the traditional understanding of the concept of a "victim" under Article 34 ECHR, significantly hindering individuals' access to Strasbourg protection. According to established case law, a complainant must demonstrate that they were directly and personally affected by the interference. In the context of mass and covert digital surveillance, meeting this requirement is often practically impossible. As Lavrysen (2015) notes, the concept of a "victim" was shaped with classical human rights violations in mind, in which interference was individual and demonstrable. In mass surveillance scenarios, individuals often do not know whether or to what extent their data has been collected or analysed. The secrecy of surveillance programs and lack of access to information mean that the requirement to demonstrate individual interference can render protection illusory.

This problem is further exacerbated in the context of transnational surveillance. Milanović points out that the combination of strict standing requirements with unclear state jurisdiction boundaries creates protection gaps, leaving individuals without an effective legal remedy (Milanović, 2011, 2015). Consequently, a system based on individual complaints cannot always respond effectively to violations of a mass or structural nature, even if they significantly affect human rights.

Significant challenges are also posed by the proportionality test applied by the ECtHR, which was developed for evaluating single, well-defined interferences in specific factual contexts. As Aharon Barak notes, the proportionality test assumes the possibility of weighing a particular interference against a specific public purpose (Barak, 2012). In mass surveillance systems, however, it is difficult to pinpoint the moment when interference occurs and to precisely define its scope. The effects of surveillance emerge gradually, through the accumulation of data and its potential future use. Fredman (2008) emphasises that traditional human rights tests struggle with structural violations that do not result from a single state action but from the functioning of entire systems. Similarly, Murphy (2017) observes that the proportionality test fails to "see the scale" of mass surveillance, focusing instead on the formal legality of the legal framework rather than the real, long-term effects on individual autonomy.

One of the most difficult consequences of digital surveillance to capture remains the chilling effect, which involves behavioural changes by individuals due to fear of monitoring. Classical analyses by Schauer already indicated that fear of potential interference can lead to self-censorship and restriction of rights, even without a direct prohibition (Schauer, 1978). In the context of digital surveillance, the chilling effect has been empirically confirmed by Penney (2016), who demonstrated that awareness of online activity monitoring reduces individuals' exercise of freedom of expression. The UN Human Rights Committee also emphasises that surveillance measures can indirectly but systematically violate freedom of expression (UN Human Rights

Committee, 2011). Although the ECtHR recognises the existence of chilling effects, this phenomenon rarely carries decisive weight in assessing violations. This is due both to evidentiary difficulties and to the indirect nature of the interference, further highlighting the limitations of the Strasbourg standard in protecting rights that are not directly violated but gradually weakened.

The digital nature of surveillance also complicates traditional notions of state jurisdiction, which underpin the ECHR protection system. Personal data is often stored outside the state's territory, processed by private entities, or transferred under international cooperation, making it difficult to attribute state responsibility. As De Hert and Papakonstantinou (2016) note, the global flow of data is in tension with the territorial model of individual rights protection. Milanović (2012, 2015) emphasises that traditional jurisdictional criteria are inadequate for digital surveillance, where control over data does not always coincide with territorial control. The UN also highlights the risk of protection gaps in cross-border data processing (OHCHR, 2014).

The analysis shows that although the Strasbourg standard plays an important role in protecting individuals from abuses by public authorities, its effectiveness in the context of digital surveillance remains limited. These limitations do not result from a lack of normative protection but from the misalignment of traditional ECHR mechanisms with the preventive, systemic, and often transnational nature of contemporary surveillance practices. The reactive ex post model, narrow definition of "victim," difficulties in applying the proportionality test to mass surveillance systems, and marginalisation of indirect effects such as chilling effects reveal structural tensions between the logic of the ECHR and the realities of digital data processing. Moreover, the territorial model of state jurisdiction is ill-suited to the global flow of information, fostering protection gaps. Consequently, human rights protection based solely on classical Strasbourg tools may prove insufficient against the challenges posed by mass digital surveillance, justifying the need to further develop ex ante standards and complementary protective mechanisms.

Recommendations for the Council of Europe and other actors

In light of the analysis of digital surveillance and its challenges for selected human rights, it is necessary to implement practical and systemic recommendations that could strengthen individual protection and supplement the existing Strasbourg standard. The proposed measures encompass normative, operational, and monitoring levels:

- Strengthening ex ante mechanisms – The Council of Europe should promote the implementation of clear and rigorous standards for the design of surveillance systems, including mandatory human rights impact assessments prior to the deployment of data collection systems; the establishment of independent oversight bodies to monitor compliance with individual rights at the design and implementation stage; time – and purpose-based limits on data processing to minimise the risk of excessive interference.
- Expanding the definition of "victim" – To enable effective access to Strasbourg protection in cases of mass and covert surveillance, the Council of Europe should recommend adopting a broader interpretation of Article 34 ECHR, encompassing individuals affected by systemic and indirect interferences; the creation of procedures allowing collective complaints or representative mechanisms to enhance practical access to protection.
- Adapting the proportionality test to the digital context – The ECtHR should develop guidelines that consider the scale of mass surveillance and the long-term effects of interference: introducing criteria for assessing risks to individual rights in big data and AI systems; analysing the cumulative effects of metadata collection and automated risk assessments.
- Recognising and accounting for the chilling effect – The Council of Europe and other international actors should recommend that evaluations of freedom of expression violations consider indirect effects of surveillance: systematic studies on the impact of digital monitoring on citizen participation in public debate; considering self-censorship as a factor limiting the realisation of human rights.
- Adapting jurisdictional frameworks to transnational surveillance – Given the global flow of data and international cooperation, it is necessary to establish mechanisms for inter-state cooperation on responsibility and information exchange; promote minimum data protection standards in cross-border data processing; develop arbitration or international tools for resolving human rights violations in the digital context.

- Education and awareness of individual rights – Strengthening citizens' competencies in data protection and digital rights: educational campaigns on the consequences of digital surveillance; informational tools enabling individuals to monitor how their data is processed.

Implementing these recommendations could significantly enhance the effectiveness of human rights protection in the digital surveillance era, complementing the ex-post response of the Strasbourg standard and mitigating systemic and transnational risks.

Conclusion

The analysis of digital surveillance indicates that contemporary technologies pose serious challenges to the traditional human rights protection system based on the European Convention on Human Rights. Mass and targeted surveillance, metadata analysis, the use of AI algorithms, and the chilling effect require reinterpretation of existing standards, adaptation of the proportionality test, and expansion of ex ante protection mechanisms. The proposed recommendations for the Council of Europe and other actors indicate directions for action that could increase the effectiveness of individual rights protection, minimise legal gaps in the Strasbourg system, and account for the global and transnational nature of digital surveillance. Implementing these solutions is essential to ensure that human rights standards keep pace with technological developments and effectively protect individuals in the digital age.

Bibliography

A. v. Norway (2009). No. 30885/06.
A.D.T. v. United Kingdom (2000). No. 35765/97.
Akkermans, B. (2020). *Transnational Data Protection and Human Rights.* Springer.
Alexy, R. (2020). *A Theory of Constitutional Rights.* Oxford University Press.
Andenas, M. (2019). *Proportionality in European Human Rights Law.* Springer.
Armonas v. Lithuania (2008). No. 10397/04.
Avilkina & Others v. Russia (2013). No. 10402/07.

Ballantyne, Davidson & McIntyre v. Canada (1993). Communication Nos. 359/1989 & 385/1989, U.N. Doc. CCPR/C/47/D/359/1989 & 385/1989/ Rev.1.
Barak, A. (2012). *Proportionality: Constitutional Rights and Their Limitations*. Cambridge University Press.
Bell, J. (2020). *Proportionality and Human Rights Law*. Oxford University Press.
Bensaid v. United Kingdom (2001). No. 44599/98.
Botta v. Italy (1998). No. 21439/93.
Big Brother Watch and Others v. the United Kingdom (2018). Nos. 58170/13, 62322/14 and 24960/15, ECHR.
Christakis, L. (2019). "The Notion of Victim in Mass Surveillance Cases at the European Court of Human Rights". *European Human Rights Law Review*, 3, 267–281.
Christian Democratic People's Party v. Moldova (2009). No. 25196/04.
Clayton, R., & Tomlinson, J. (2022). *The Law of Human Rights* (6th ed.). Oxford University Press.
Clough, E. (2020). "Chilling Effects of Digital Surveillance on Freedom of Expression". *Journal of Law and Society*, 47(2), 233–258.
Couderc Hachette Filipacciés v. France (2012). No. 40454/07.
Council of Europe (2023). *Guide on Article 8 of the European Convention on Human Rights*. Council of Europe Publishing.
Craven, M. (2018). *The European Convention on Human Rights: Achievements, Problems and Prospects*. Oxford University Press.
Dammann v. Switzerland (2006). No. 77544/01.
De Hert, P., & Papakonstantinou, V. (2016). "The New General Data Protection Regulation: Still a Sound System for the Protection of Individuals?" *Computer Law & Security Review*, 32(2), 179–194.
De Hert, P., & Papakonstantinou, V. (2018). "The New General Data Protection Regulation: Still a Sound System for the Protection of Fundamental Rights?" *International Data Privacy Law*, 8(2), 1–23.
De La Flor Cabrera v. Spain (2014). No. 37249/10.
den Hertog, L. (2021). *Digital Sovereignty, Jurisdiction, and Human Rights*. Routledge.
Dudgeon v. United Kingdom (1985). No. 7525/76.
Editorial Board of Pravoye Delo & Shtekel v. Ukraine (2011). No. 33044/05.
Fáber v. Hungary (2012). No. 40721/08.
Flinkkälä & Others v. Finland (2010). No. 25576/04.

Fredman, S. (2008). *Human Rights Transformed: Positive Rights and Positive Duties*. Oxford University Press.

Friedl v. Austria (1994). No. 15210/89.

Goodwin v. United Kingdom (1996). No. 17488/90.

Gough v. United Kingdom (1980). No. 10244/83; 2014, No. 49327/11.

Greenleaf, G. (2020). "Global Data Privacy Laws 2020: 150 Countries and Counting". *Privacy Laws & Business International Report*, 158, 10–13.

Guja v. Moldova (2008). No. 14277/04.

Gutwirth, S., & Poullet, Y. (2019). "The Right to Privacy in the Digital Age: Ex Post Protection and Its Limits". *Computer Law & Security Review*, 35(2), 1–12.

Handyside v. United Kingdom (1976). No. 5493/72.

Haguenauer v. France (2010). No. 34050/05.

Harris, D. (2017). *Freedom of Expression and the Chilling Effect in European Law*. Oxford University Press.

Harris, D., O'Boyle, M., & Warbrick, C. (2018). *Law of the European Convention on Human Rights* (3rd ed.). Oxford University Press.

Hilton v. United Kingdom (1988). No. 11464/85.

Karakó v. Hungary (2009). No. 39311/05.

Kaye, D. (2019). *Report of the Special Rapporteur on the Promotion and Protection of the Right to Freedom of Opinion and Expression* (A/HRC/41/35). United Nations Human Rights Council.

Khelili v. Switzerland (2011). No. 37852/04.

Klass & Others v. Germany (1978). No. 5029/71.

Korff, D. (2012). "The Standard Approach under Articles 8–11 ECHR and Surveillance". London School of Economics and Political Science.

Kuner, C. (2020a). *Transborder Data Flows and Data Privacy Law*. Oxford University Press.

Kuner, C. (2020b). *The European Union and the Regulation of Digital Surveillance: Challenges for Privacy and Human Rights*. Cambridge University Press.

Kuner, C. (2020c). *European Data Protection Law: Corporate Compliance and Regulation*. Oxford University Press.

Kuner, C. (2021). "Extraterritoriality and Data Protection in Human Rights Law". *International Data Privacy Law*, 11(2), 103–115.

Lavrysen, L. (2015). "The Concept of 'Victim' in Strasbourg Case Law". *European Human Rights Law Review*, 4, 353–368.

Liberty and Others v. United Kingdom (2008). No. 58243/00.

Lyon, D. (2018). *The Culture of Surveillance: Watching as a Way of Life*. Polity Press.

Milanović, M. (2011). *Extraterritorial Application of Human Rights Treaties: Law, Principles, and Policy*. Oxford University Press.
Milanović, M. (2015). "Human Rights Treaties and Foreign Surveillance: Privacy in the Digital Age". *Harvard International Law Journal*, *56*(1), 81–146.
Moeckli, D. (2020). *International Human Rights Law* (3rd ed.). Oxford University Press.
Murphy, C. (2017). "The Problem of Mass Surveillance and Proportionality". *European Human Rights Law Review*, 3, 305–320.
Murray, A. K. (2021). "Indirect Human Rights Violations in the Era of Mass Surveillance". *Human Rights Quarterly*, 43(2), 312–340.
Nielsen & Johnsen v. Norway (1999). No. 23118/93.
Niemietz v. Germany (1992). No. 13710/88.
O'Flaherty, M. (2019). *Human Rights Law*. Routledge.
Öllinger v. Austria (2006). No. 76900/01.
Penney, J. (2016). "Chilling Effects: Online Surveillance and Wikipedia Use". *Berkeley Technology Law Journal*, 31(1), 117–182.
Pollicino, O. (2019). "Digital Sovereignty and Jurisdictional Challenges". *European Law Review*, 44(3), 397–414.
Pfeifer v. Austria (2007). No. 12556/03.
Prager & Oberschlick v. Austria (1995). No. 15974/90.
Reklos & Davourlis v. Greece (2009). No. 1234/05.
Rotaru v. Romania (2000). No. 28341/95.
S.H. & Others v. Austria (2011). No. 57813/00.
Sanchez Cardenas v. Norway (2007). No. 45963/99.
Shvydka v. Ukraine (2014). No. 17888/12.
Starzyk, K. (2020). "Challenges of Digital Surveillance for the European Court of Human Rights". *Human Rights Law Review*, 20(3), 487–512.
Szabó and Vissy v. Hungary (2016). No. 37138/14.
Sürek v. Turkey (1999). No. 26682/95.
Telegraaf Media Nederland Landelijke Media B.V. & Others v. Netherlands (2001). No. 34085/96.
The Sunday Times v. United Kingdom (1979). No. 6538/74.
Uzun v. Germany (2010). No. 35623/05.
Vajnai v. Hungary (2008). No. 33629/06.
Weber & Saravia v. Germany (2006). No. 54934/00.
United Nations Human Rights Committee (2011). *General Comment No. 34: Article 19 – Freedoms of opinion and expression* (CCPR/C/GC/34).

United Nations Office of the High Commissioner for Human Rights (2014). *The right to privacy in the digital age* (A/HRC/27/37).

van den Berg, S. L. (2021). "Proportionality in Mass Data Collection: Challenges for the European Court of Human Rights". *Human Rights Law Journal*, 41(1), 23–45.

Youth Initiative for Human Rights v. Serbia (2013). No. 48135/06.

Zakharov v. Russia (2015). No. 47143/06.

Zuboff, S. (2019). *The Age of Surveillance Capitalism: The Fight for a Human Future at the New Frontier of Power.* PublicAffairs.

AI as a co-creator: How artificial intelligence is transforming the gaming industry

Igor Walczak[1]

ABSTRACT

This article examines the role of artificial intelligence (AI) as a co-creator in the process of developing computer games. Based on a review of literature, industry reports, and articles on internet portals, the author describes various ways in which game developers use AI. An overview of the various methods of using AI shows that this technology has a significant impact on the gaming industry, accelerating and automating many activities and personalising the player experience. The examples of AI tools described emphasise the co-creative nature of this technology, pointing to its role in the development of innovative methods of game creation. The author emphasises that while AI in the gaming industry brings many benefits, challenges must also be taken into account, including those related to protecting player privacy, protecting jobs, and preserving human creativity. In addition, he reflects on the future of the industry, noting that AI has the potential to further transform it. However, fully exploiting this potential will require a responsible approach on the part of developers, who must take player expectations into account.

Keywords: Video games, artificial intelligence, co-creator, technology, gaming

Introduction

The video games market is constantly evolving and becoming increasingly important. This is demonstrated, among other things, by the global revenues generated by this industry, which are growing year on year. It currently exceeds the combined revenues of both music and film industries, which undoubtedly highlights the importance of this medium today (Newzoo, 2023, p. 17). This shows that video games are not only a source of entertainment for millions of people, but also an important sector of the economy. It is therefore no surprise that, with the growing role of artificial intelligence, it is increasingly being used in the context of video games.

Video games are one of the areas where AI will potentially have the greatest impact. Changes may affect both technical issues related to production and the way narratives and experiences are created for players. Currently, games

1 ORCID iD: 0009-0003-1963–8354

are not only a form of entertainment, but also an effective communication tool. This is due to the fact that they are a very versatile medium that can be used in many areas. They can be educational, artistic, and can also be used as a marketing tool. Sometimes, individual titles address important social and political issues, thereby influencing the attitudes and awareness of players. The importance of video games in terms of their impact on culture and society, especially among young demographic groups, cannot be overestimated. The growing importance of artificial intelligence in the gaming industry and the potential that lies in this technology is therefore worth noting.

A co-creator is a person who makes a creative contribution to a work, while co-creation means that the final outcome results from the contributions of more than one person (Banasiuk, 2012, p. 15). The question then arises as to whether we can talk about co-creation in the case of artificial intelligence. This is undoubtedly a very complex question to which it is difficult to give a clear answer. On the one hand, AI has no personality and is not a living being. Its actions are dictated solely by algorithms and data on the basis of which it has been trained. Its "creativity" results from complex computational processes that merely mimic human thinking. It would follow that AI is not a co-creator in the traditional sense of the word. On the other hand, however, it cannot be denied that the creative potential of artificial intelligence is enormous. Given its advanced capabilities, which can make a significant contribution to the game development process, it would be reasonable to consider AI a co-creator.

Methodology

The article uses several complementary research methods. First, it is based on a review of academic literature, which provides theoretical background on artificial intelligence and its role in creative processes. Second, the author analyses industry reports and policy documents, allowing the discussion to reflect current developments in the video game industry and existing legal frameworks.

In addition, the study draws on case-based examples of games and AI tools to show how artificial intelligence is used in practice. Selected online sources and professional publications are also examined to capture on-going debates within the industry. Together, these methods make it possible to present a broad and up-to-date overview of how AI is transforming game development, while also addressing its main opportunities and challenges.

From simple algorithms to dynamic worlds

It is impossible to discuss artificial intelligence without defining the term. The most popular definition of artificial intelligence is that it is the ability of machines and computer systems to exhibit human skills such as reasoning, learning, planning, and problem-solving (Zhang, 2021, pp. 1–2). In the context of video games, artificial intelligence can be described as a set of techniques, tools, and programming methods that aim to simulate intelligent behaviour of characters independent of the player and to create a dynamic and responsive[2] game environment, as well as content intended for inclusion in the game (Yannakakis & Togelius, 2018, pp. 23–25).

It should be noted that the presence of artificial intelligence in video games is not a new phenomenon. The origins of this technology date back to the 1950s, when the first experiments with AI algorithms began to be integrated into simple games (Xia et al., 2020, p. 505). Over the years, the development of AI in games has evolved from basic rules to more complex techniques. Initially, AI was limited to the use of simple algorithms that were encoded directly into the game. Over time, techniques such as behaviour trees and more advanced algorithms that learned from the player's actions began to appear (Sagredo-Olivenza et al., 2019, p. 1). A breakthrough in this regard was the game *Halo 2* (2004), in which the characters' actions were exceptionally complex for its time. Enemies were able to adjust their behaviour based on specific factors, such as the player's position and actions.

Today, techniques such as machine learning and procedural generation are used in game development. They enable the creation of even more complex, realistic, and diverse experiences for players (Summerville et al., 2018, pp. 257–258). Particular attention should be paid to generative artificial intelligence, a technology that enables the automatic creation of content such as graphics, animations, and music by learning from input data (Epstein et al., 2023, pp. 1110–1111). Due to its specific nature and the possibilities it offers,

---

2 Responsiveness in this case means the ability of the game environment to react to the player's actions.

it has the potential to transform the gaming industry in the near future. It is capable of facilitating and significantly accelerating many activities related to game design and development.

Versatile applications of AI in video games

One of the elements that will be affected by generative artificial intelligence is the design of independent characters, or NPCs (*non-player characters*). Such characters are currently based on pre-prepared scripts. Their speech and behaviour are therefore often quite limited. One response to this is a prototype of generative AI called NEO NPC, developed by Ubisoft. The main goal of this project is to enable more natural interactions between players and NPCs (O'Brien, 2024). Through the use of advanced algorithms, the behaviour of non-player characters can be more complex and realistic. Machine learning, in turn, allows these behaviours to be adapted to the game environment and the player's actions. As a result, each encounter with such a character can look completely different, which has a positive effect on immersion[3] and replayability[4]. The statements generated by artificial intelligence do not negatively affect the authenticity of the game world, as they fit within the framework imposed by the scriptwriters. In a sense, they create the personality of the characters on which the artificial intelligence operates.

In addition to supporting character design, AI has the ability to create narratives with an unprecedented level of interactivity. There is no doubt that storytelling plays a key role in computer games, especially when it comes to player engagement. Unlike traditional narratives, those created with the support of AI are able to respond to players' actions in real time, offering personalised experiences. Algorithms, based primarily on natural language processing (NLP), can analyse player behaviour and preferences in real time to customise dialogues, characters, and storylines. An example of a game that has successfully implemented this solution is *The Elder Scrolls V: Skyrim*. In this title, algorithms can dynamically generate missions tailored to the player's level and location. Text-based games such as *Dungeon AI*, which allow

---

[3] Immersion in the context of video games means being deeply engaged in the world and atmosphere of a given game.

[4] Replayability can be defined simply as the desire to play a given title again.

players to create unique stories based on prompts they use are also good examples[5]. The biggest challenge in creating narratives with AI is ensuring consistency. For the narrative to be engaging and logical, algorithms must not only respond to the player's current decisions but also remember previous choices and consistently develop specific storylines.

Artificial intelligence is used in the design and generation of virtual worlds and the elements within them. One of the methods that makes this possible is the aforementioned procedural generation. It involves creating a game environment, i.e. landscapes, buildings, fauna, and flora, using algorithms. These algorithms operate on the basis of specific rules and predefined patterns. This method largely eliminates the need to manually model each element of the world. A prime example of its use is the game *No Man's Sky*. The gameplay focuses on exploring space, which consists of countless procedurally generated planets. According to the developers, the number of planets that can be generated is as high as 18 trillion. Each of them is unique in terms of both the environment and the creatures that inhabit it (Tait & Nelson, 2021, p. 695). It should be noted that procedural generation is not synonymous with artificial intelligence. One could argue that this is the case with *No Man's Sky*, because despite generating game elements using algorithms, the entire process lacks the characteristics typical of this technology, such as machine learning or adapting to the player's actions in real time. Nevertheless, it shows the potential of this technology, which, with the support of artificial intelligence can increase its capabilities. This will allow for the aforementioned real-time responses to player decisions, as well as greater control over the generated content. It will enable developers to edit and modify it if necessary. In addition, AI-generated worlds can be more realistic, and the ecosystems within them can appear more credible and authentic.

There are a number of AI tools that can greatly simplify the process of creating graphic assets[6]. Programs based on GAN (*Generative Adversarial Network*) technology are capable of generating almost photorealistic images based on patterns presented to them beforehand (Ergen, 2023, p. 58). Thanks

---

5 A prompt is a phrase that serves as an instruction or command for an artificial intelligence system.

6 In the context of computer games, assets are all resources, such as graphics, sounds, or animations, which are used to build the game world.

to this technology, the time needed to design graphics can be reduced to just a few seconds. This is particularly important in the production of games, which require a large number of graphic elements, each of which requires special preparation. Artificial intelligence can also be used for resolution scaling, as exemplified by Nvidia's DLSS (*Deep Learning Super Sampling*) technology. It uses real-time machine learning to improve image quality. The principle of operation is based on analysing the graphics and estimating how they should look in higher resolution. As a result, despite the lower initial resolution, the output image is clearer and more detailed. All this without the computational load that would result from the process of generating a better-quality image (Smith, 2023).

In addition to graphics-related aspects, AI can also assist creators with issues related to the sound design of their productions. AI tools allow for the composition of complex musical pieces that can be used as game soundtracks (Ramdurai & Adhithya, 2023, pp. 4–5). Moreover, such tools are capable of generating a variety of sound effects that would require a great deal of time and resources to record in the traditional way. The ability to generate sounds in real time is particularly important. This allows for dynamic interaction with the environment, including non-player characters. An example of such application is a modification for *The Elder Scrolls V: Skyrim*, using Inworld AI and ElevenLabs software. It allows players to engage in dialogue with NPCs, contributing to a significant increase in immersion and realism. Players can choose between voice communication using a microphone and typing their lines into a chat window. Characters have specific personalities that determine what they say. This ensures that the topics of conversation do not go beyond the game world, thus disrupting the consistency of the gameplay.

Another area where artificial intelligence can assist game developers is quality control, which includes game testing activities. Traditional game testing involves, among other things, repeatedly playing through specific parts of the game to identify various types of errors. However, testers can use AI-powered bots to perform repetitive tasks for them. With its ability to process natural language, AI is able to analyse player behaviour and gameplay feedback and suggest solutions based on this analysis. Testers can also use AI tools to protect against hackers and cheaters in online games by detecting unusual behaviour in gameplay (Mascellino, 2023).

New opportunities for game developers

Artificial intelligence is playing an increasingly important role in various fields, and its use in video game production is becoming more and more visible. In this context, AI is no longer just a tool for creating more intelligent opponents or realistic animations, but is becoming an active co-creator, influencing all aspects of the creative process. This has a number of consequences for both the entire creative process and the medium of games itself. Firstly, AI tools allow for a significant acceleration and streamlining of this process, which results from the automation of a large part of the tasks. Developers can devote the additional time to other aspects of production. Automation also reduces production costs, which is particularly important given that they are already very high. The savings can be used, for example, for promotional activities. Artificial intelligence brings an unprecedented level of interactivity and realism to video games. The use of machine-learning-based tools allows for the creation of immersive environments, individually tailored to the recipient. This introduces elements of authenticity and unpredictability to the games, which have a positive impact on player engagement.

Artificial intelligence is no longer the domain of large corporations, and the democratisation of this technology has a number of consequences, including in the context of the computer games industry. Tools that were previously reserved only for large developers are now also available to smaller and independent developers who do not have huge budgets. This significantly contributes to lowering the barrier to market entry for them. The result may be increased competition, which in turn may lead to greater diversity among new games. This is associated with attracting new audiences and increasing the value of the entire market. It also encourages innovation, as a larger number of creators means fiercer competition, which will encourage them to continuously improve and refine their products.

The democratisation of AI may also affect the inclusivity of the computer games industry. With easier access to advanced technologies, more people with diverse experiences have the opportunity to create them. As a result, more titles may begin to emerge that address socially important topics and represent different points of view. In the broader perspective, this may lead to the creation of a more open community of players who enjoy diverse and inclusive experiences in games that not only entertain but also educate and build social awareness.

Analysis of threats and challenges

The use of artificial intelligence in the creation of video games also presents a number of challenges. One of these is the bias of algorithms resulting from distorted or limited data on which they are trained. The use of such algorithms in character design can, for example, perpetuate certain stereotypes or discriminate against specific social groups (Melhart et al., 2024, pp. 84–85). It is the role of developers to counteract this by training algorithms using diverse and inclusive data sets.

Another challenge is related to automation, which poses a real risk of job loss for many professionals in the industry. Creative professions, including graphic designers in particular, are most at risk. They may be gradually replaced by AI software, which may lead to a reduction in the need to hire artists and designers. Game testers also face the risk of being replaced by AI tools that are capable of detecting errors and technical problems. In response to these changes, employees in the gaming industry will have to consider the need to adapt to the new reality. One option may be to retrain for specialties that are not as susceptible to automation. In addition, it will be important to continuously develop one's skills, dictated by the needs of the industry (Richardson, 2024). It is important that both employees and employers are aware of this issue and work together to protect jobs.

The implementation of AI in creative processes also involves the collection and analysis of large amounts of player data. There is a risk of privacy and data security breaches if appropriate practices of transparency, secure data storage, and user consent are not followed (Richardson, 2024).

In the context of challenges, it is also worth mentioning the threat to the artistic dimension of games resulting from the potential limitation of human creativity. AI tools have unlimited potential when it comes to generating content, but they lack human imagination and the ability to feel emotions. As a result, games may lose their individual character and depth. People bring their own experiences to games and are guided by specific values and sensibilities when working on them. As a result, games have a unique character manifested in nuances that artificial intelligence is unable to reproduce. It is important to maintain a balance between undoubtedly useful technology and human creativity, which cannot be replaced.

How creators and players perceive AI in games

Representatives of the gaming industry have mixed opinions on the use of generative artificial intelligence. A survey was conducted as part of the Game Developers Conference, in which over 3,000 developers took part. It showed that 31 % of respondents use generative AI in their work. In turn, 18 % responded that they do not use it themselves, but other people in their workplace do (GDC, 2024, pp. 12–15). This means that almost half of the respondents work in companies where generative AI is used. The survey also shows that AI is most commonly used in finance, marketing, PR, production, and management, and least commonly in departments dealing with story-telling, graphic and sound design, and quality control. It is worth noting that not all companies allow their employees to use generative AI tools. It turns out that 12 % of respondents said that their company has a policy prohibiting the use of generative AI. Another 7 % indicated that certain tools are allowed, while others are not. In contrast, 2 % of respondents admitted that they are required to use AI in their work. Most respondents said that their companies do not have a set policy on generative AI or that the use of these tools is solely up to the employee (GDC, 2024, pp. 12–15). The overall tone of this research is that creators' opinions on the impact of AI on the industry are divided. Those who work in business or marketing departments believe that it will be positive. On the other hand, creative employees and those responsible for quality control have negative feelings. Respondents agreed on the impact on ethics in the industry, with as many as 84 % expressing moderate or significant concern about ethical issues, while only 12 % said they had no concerns (GDC, 2024, pp. 12–15).

In the discussion on this topic, the opinion of the players themselves is equally important. Research shows that gamers are optimistic about the benefits that artificial intelligence can bring, provided that the technology is used responsibly (National Research Group, 2024). As many as 60 % of gamers believe that AI will have a positive impact on the industry, while only 11 % expect negative effects. The gaming community is aware of the potential risks associated with the implementation of generative AI in the industry. Only 25 % believe that studios should fully commit to using this technology. The majority, 58 %, see AI as a useful tool that must be used cautiously and responsibly. Gamers are also aware of the ethical issues surrounding AI and intellectual property. As many as 80 % say that studios using AI-based tools should take steps to ensure that AI does not plagiarise the work of artists, voice actors, writers, and other creative professionals (National Research Group, 2024).

Reflections on the future

As artificial intelligence develops, more and more attention will be focused on the legal regulations covering this technology. The rules established by lawmakers will define how artificial intelligence will be used in various industries, including the computer games industry. This means that companies will face challenges they have not encountered before. In March 2024, the European Union adopted a regulation called the AI Act, which establishes a common regulatory framework for member states. In general, the AI Act takes a risk-based approach. Regulations depend on the capabilities of a particular tool and the risks associated with it (Tartaro, 2023, pp. 148–149). One category is general-purpose AI systems (GPAIs), which include tools used in the creation of video games. All providers of tools classified in this category are required to comply with European Union copyright law. In addition, the AI Act requires full transparency regarding the operating principles and data used in training specific AI models (Tartaro, 2023, pp. 148–149). In the United States, on the other hand, the Copyright Office is responsible for legislative issues related to generative artificial intelligence. Under US copyright law, content created using generative artificial intelligence is not protected because it was not created by a human being (Han, 2023, p. 3). As a result, many companies may limit their use of AI tools due to fears about the risks associated with insufficient protection. When discussing the future of AI regulations, it is important to bear in mind that this technology is still evolving and undergoing constant change. Lawmakers must take this dynamic into account when creating new regulations, which should be continuously updated and adapted to the prevailing realities.

Reflection on the future of the gaming industry and the role that artificial intelligence will play in it points to revolutionary changes in both the game development process and the player experience itself. AI has the potential to significantly facilitate the work of developers and increase the realism and immersion of games, as well as introduce completely new genres and forms of gameplay. In the future, AI may further simplify the game production process by automating additional tasks. Clint Hocking, a Canadian computer game designer and director, predicts that by 2032, AI will be able to create games from scratch, based only on short prompts, with virtually no human involvement (McKnight, 2024). This would revolutionise the way games are produced, allowing developers to quickly test new ideas. The development of AI will also affect the player experience, offering even more realistic and immersive games. Furthermore, AI could enable the creation of entirely new genres and types of games that would be impossible to create without this technology. The future of gaming will likely also include the integration of AI with virtual reality (VR) and augmented reality (AR) technology. Such a combination could provide unprecedented experiences, immersing players in virtual worlds on an unprecedented scale.

Conclusion

Artificial intelligence has the potential to revolutionise the gaming industry on many levels. The automation of the game development process, the ability to generate games using AI based on prompts, the creation of more immersive experiences, and integration with VR and AR technology are just some of the possible changes. The future of gaming will undoubtedly be exciting and full of innovation thanks to the dynamic development of this technology. Video games are a medium to be reckoned with these days. By combining entertainment, art, and technology, they have enormous cultural significance. Their global popularity and presence in everyday life make them an important part of contemporary culture. The development of artificial intelligence has a significant impact on the evolution of this medium. Thanks to its participation in the creative process, artificial intelligence plays the role of a co-creator, and its presence will become increasingly visible over time. This brings both benefits and risks that creators must be aware of. It is important to keep ethical issues in mind and maintain a balance between technology and humans. It is human input, imagination, and passion that make games unique. It is therefore crucial that artificial intelligence serve as a tool that supports, rather than replaces, human creativity. We can only hope that collaboration between humans and AI will result in the creation of many truly unique titles.

Bibliography

Banasiuk, J. (2012). *Co-creation and Its Effects in Copyright Law*. Warsaw: Wolters Kluwer.

Ergen, İ. (2023). "Generating Video Game Characters Using StyleGAN2." *Journal of Awareness, 8*(1), 57–61. <https://doi.org/10.26809/joa.1974>

Epstein, Z., Hertzmann, A., Herman, L., Mahari, R., Frank, M. R., Groh, M., Schroeder, H., Smith, A., Akten, M., Fjeld, J., Farid, H., Leach, N., Pentland, A., & Russakovsky, O. (2023). "Art and the Science of Generative AI." *Science, 380*(6650), 1110–1111. <DOI: 10.1126/science.adh4451>

Game Developers Conference (GDC) (2024). *GDC 2024 State of the Game Industry Report*. <https://reg.gdconf.com/state-of-game-industry-2024> (July 20, 2025).

Han, T. (2023). "On the Copyright of Content Generated by Artificial Intelligence." *SHS Web of Conferences*, 178.

Mascellino, A. (2023). "AI Video Game Testing: Is it a Turbo Boost for Quality Assurance?" Techopedia.com. <https://www.techopedia.com/ai-video-game-testing-is-it-a-turbo-boost-for-quality-assurance> (July 21, 2025).

McKnight, T. (2024). "What's Next for AI in Video Games?" Humble Bundle Blog. <https://blog.humblebundle.com/2024/02/01/whats-next-for-ai-in-video-games/> (July 23, 2025).

Melhart, D., Togelius, J., Mikkelsen, B., Holmgård, C., & Yannakakis, G. N. (2024). "The Ethics of AI in Games." *IEEE Transactions on Affective Computing* 15, 1.

National Research Group (2024). *Pressing Play on AI: A Game-Changing Power-Up?* pp. 3–6. https://assets.ctfassets.net/4ivt4uy3jinr/3beozVj5ZfyoDL37nKJTz1/f6413195dcb77ee639cd884d716a53c3/NRG_Pressing_Play_on_AI__2023.pdf

Newzoo, *Global Games Market Report* (2023). <https://newzoo.com/resources/trend-reports/newzoo-global-games-market-report-2023-free-version> (July 16, 2025).

O'Brien, L. (2024). "How Ubisoft's New Generative AI Prototype Changes the Narrative for NPCs." Ubisoft.com. <https://news.ubisoft.com/en-us/article/5qXdxhshJBXoanFZApdG3L/how-ubisofts-new-generative-ai-prototype-changes-the-narrative-for-npcs> (July 18, 2025).

Ramdurai, B., & Adhithya, P. (2023). "The Impact, Advancements and Applications of Generative AI." *SSRG International Journal of Computer Science and Engineering, 10*(6):1-8.

Richardson, T. (2024). "How AI is Fuelling Uncertainty for Game Developers." BBC.com. <https://www.bbc.com/news/articles/cl44mv0jnv5o> (July 22, 2025).
Sagredo-Olivenza, I., Gomez-Martin, P. P., Gomez-Martin, M. A., & Gonzalez-Calero, P. A. (2019). "Trained Behavior Trees: Programming by Demonstration to Support AI Game Designers." *IEEE Transactions on Games* 11, 1.
Smith, M. (2023). "What Is DLSS and Why Does it Matter for Gaming?" IGN.com. <https://www.ign.com/articles/what-is-nvidia-dlss-meaning> (July 19, 2025).
Summerville, A., Snodgrass, S., Guzdial, M., Holmgård, C., Hoover, A. K., Isaksen, A., Nealen, A., & Togelius, J. (2018). "Procedural Content Generation via Machine Learning (PCGML)." *IEEE Transactions on Games* 10, 3.
Tait, E., & Nelson, I. (2021). "Nonscalability and Generating Digital Outer Space Natures in No Man's Sky." *Environment and Planning E: Nature and Space* 5, 2.
Tartaro, A. (2023). "Regulating by Standards: Current Progress and Main Challenges in the Standardization of Artificial Intelligence in Support of the AI Act." *European Journal of Privacy Law and Technologies* 1.
Xia, B., Ye, X., & Abuassba, A. O. (2020). "Recent Research on AI in Games." *2020 International Wireless Communications and Mobile Computing (IWCMC)*.
Yannakakis, G., & Togelius, J. (2018). *Artificial Intelligence and Games*. Cham: Springer.
Zhang, L., Pan, Y., Wu, X., & Skibniewski, M. (2021). *Artificial Intelligence in Construction Engineering and Management*. Singapore: Springer.

MANAGEMENT IN DIGITAL TIMES

Edited by Piotr Olaf Żylicz

Vol. 1 Krzysztof Kasianiuk / Bohdan Szklarski / Piotr Olaf Żylicz (eds.): Failed Leadership. 2021.

Vol. 2 Piotr Olaf Żylicz / Vartika Dutta / Rathish Bhatt: Mapping Manager Development. Current and Upcoming Trends. 2023.

Vol. 3 Krzysztof Wasilewski (ed.): Digital Humanities and Digital Skills in the Future of Work. 2025.

Vol. 4 Krzysztof Wasilewski / Tomasz Królikowski (eds.): The Future of Work. An Interdisciplinary Approach. 2026.

www.peterlang.com

Kolibri 360 GmbH
Ferdinand-Jühlke-Straße 7
99095 Erfurt, Deutschland
produktsicherheit@kolibri360.de

Druck:
CPI Druckdienstleistungen GmbH
im Auftrag der
Kolibri 360 GmbH
Ferdinand-Jühlke-Str. 7
99095 Erfurt